Hispanic and Lusophone Voices of Africa

edited by

David Mongor-Lizarrabengoa

Wor-Wic Community College in Salisbury, Maryland

and

Sarita Naa Akuye Addy

Canadian Center for Diversity and Inclusion

Series in Literary Studies

VERNON PRESS

www.vernonpress.com

In the Americas:
Vernon Press
1000 N West Street, Suite 1200
Wilmington, Delaware, 19801
United States

In the rest of the world:
Vernon Press
C/Sancti Espiritu 17,
Malaga, 29006
Spain

Series in Literary Studies

Library of Congress Control Number: 2022935707

ISBN: 978-1-64889-568-5

Also available: 978-1-64889-426-8 [Hardback]; 978-1-64889-481-7 [PDF, E-Book]

Table of Contents

Introduction

David Mongor-Lizarrabengoa

Wor-Wic Community College in Salisbury, Maryland

This volume began life as a panel proposal for the 2019 Northeast Modern Language (NeMLA) Convention hosted by Georgetown University. When choosing panel topics of the NeMLA conventions, I typically choose a topic that often is underrepresented in Hispanic and/or Lusophone literary and film scholarship, but with this approach, there are usually fewer submissions than for a panel on a more mainstream topic. After some debate, I opted for a panel titled "Hispanic and Lusophone Literatures of Africa." Equatorial Guinea was grouped in with the Lusophone nations on the continent as I worried that without its inclusion, I would not receive enough proposals to run the panel. To my complete surprise, over ten submissions were received which forced the panel to be broken into two sessions, one on Lusophone Africa and another just on Equatorial Guinea. At the conference, both panels were well-received by the audience with one person commenting that in the twenty-five years he had been attended the NeMLA convention, he was amazed that for the first time, there had been a panel dedicated exclusively to Equatorial Guinean literature. With such positive reception, I knew this topic needed to be explored further as there is definitely a gap in this area of academic publishing. Shortly after the conference, a representative from Vernon Press reached out to me asking if I would be willing to edit a volume on my conference topic to which I gladly accepted the task.

If one were to search courses in Spanish and Portuguese graduate and undergraduate programs in the United States, the lists of courses offered will likely contain numerous courses on Spain, Portugal, Brazil, and the other major nations in Latin America. Equatorial Guinea and Lusophone African countries may not appear at all, and if they do, there may only be one or two courses covering the literature, cinema, and linguistics of these nations. With regard to Equatorial Guinea, it is the only African nation where Spanish is an official language with about 68% of the population being fluent in it. When people think of countries where Spanish is spoken, they usually think of Spain and some Latin American states, completely oblivious to the fact a Spanish-speaking nation exists in Africa. Prior to the 1990s, volumes of literature written in Spanish rarely featured Equatorial Guinean writers. The *Afro-Hispanic Review* and a few international conferences helped to expose members of the academic community to scholarship on writers from Equatorial Guinea. In terms of cinema production, the country has not been known for its film industry. In 2014, the first international feature film shot in Equatorial Guinea, *Where the Road Runs Out* premiered at the San Diego International Film Festival, winning two awards. Since then there have been a handful of new films produced in the nation. If directors and filmmakers in the nation receive government support and can find funding resources elsewhere, the nation has the potential to create a small-scale film industry that could produce very unique films compared to the output of Spain and Latin American countries.

In terms of Lusophone Africa, Angola boasts approximately twenty million[1] speakers of Portuguese. In Mozambique, there are about 12 million Portuguese speakers. Cabo Verde is home to about 500,000 Lusophones. Roughly 950,000 residents of Guinea-Bissau can speak Portuguese. Lastly, Portuguese is spoken by about 120,000 citizens of the island nation of São Tomé and Príncipe.[2] Undoubtedly, Brazil is by far home to the most speakers of Portuguese with over 200 million, but when compared to Portugal's 10 million speakers, the five African nations comprise a sizeable chunk of the world's Lusophone population. Whereas Equatorial Guinean writers struggled to gain recognition in the academic world, Lusophone African writers have not experienced as much adversity as there have been a handful of volumes published on Luso-African works along with many journal articles. Despite this exposure amongst the research community, there is still a need to research and explore the voices that emerge from the five Lusophone nations in Africa.

This book seeks to explore literary texts and films from Equatorial Guinea and Portuguese-speaking Africa: Angola, Mozambique, Cabo Verde, Guinea-Bissau, and São Tomé and Príncipe. While fiction and film operate using different discourses, they both involve storytelling, character development, and thematic messages so there is some overlap. In the case of the nations represented in the volume, many do not have extensive film production histories; hence, both film and fiction are presented in this text. This volume has two principal aims. First, this book seeks to acquaint readers that speak English with works of fiction and films from these six African nations. Secondly, this volume adds to the scholarship already published on Equatorial Guinea and Lusophone Africa. As stated, these nations have often been overshadowed by the major players in the Spanish and Portuguese-speaking world. This volume is not an exhaustive study of the literature or film production of these

---

[1] The figures in this paragraph include native speakers of the language, those that speak Portuguese-based creole languages, and residents who speak Portuguese fluently as a second language.

[2] Portuguese is also a co-official language in Equatorial Guinea, but it is not widely spoken there.

nations. The various authors have chosen to work with more contemporary works that were written/filmed in Spanish and Portuguese. While the various chapters may mention texts and literary movements from the past, the emphasis is placed on post-independence works. In addition, no texts or movies made in the numerous indigenous African languages of these nations are featured.

The essays contained in this volume highlight some of the most important texts and films to be produced in Equatorial Guinea and Lusophone Africa. The authors of these chapters come from diverse academic backgrounds so there are different ways the texts and films are engaged. Each chapter explores one or more texts/films, the social context surrounding the society it represents, and its reception by the public. In the first chapter, Sarita Addy examines Donato Ndongo-Bidyogo's *Los poderes de la tempestad* (1997), one of the most well-known and widely read narratives about Equatorial Guinea. The novel offers a sharp, candid criticism of colonial and postcolonial systems of oppression in Equatorial Guinea. The novel's evocation of resistance against the authoritarianism of the Nguemist regime also encompasses what resistance meant to the allies of the dictator. In this chapter, she analyzes, Ada, a female paramilitary officer who is complicit with the dictator, and argues that her alliance with the dictator within the social and political degeneration of Nguema's Equatorial Guinea is a kind of resistance against neo-colonialism and traditional Fang patriarchy. While the novel frames her resistance as anti-colonial, anti-patriarchal sentiments are revealed that point to double oppression from both Nguemist and colonialist ideologies of the Guinean woman.

The remaining chapters in the volume engage texts and films from Lusophone Africa. The second chapter, written by Paulo Rodrigues Ferreira, analyzes *Comissão das Lágrimas* (2011), a novel by Lobo Antunes focusing on Angola. Having served as a military doctor in the Portuguese Colonial War, it is no surprise that he has written extensively about the downfall of Portugal's colonial presence in Africa. Ferreria seeks to examine how Antunes engages colonial and postcolonial ideas with specific emphasis on how one's experiences impact memories of past events. In his discussion of *Comissão das Lágrimas*, he explores the mentally challenged character, Cristiana, who is traumatized by her past and recounts the horrors carried out by her father, a member of the so-called Comissão das Lágrimas. Supposedly, an organization was created in 1977 to persecute and arrest the intellectuals involved in a failed coup to overthrow Agostinho Neto's government. The chapter seeks to answer several key questions including: how do Lobo Antunes's literary techniques help him to recount historical events? How can fiction help readers to apprehend the complexities of history? What are the frontiers between reality and fiction in his oeuvre, especially in *Comissão das Lágrimas*?

The third chapter, by Martha Mzite and Margret Chipara, offers a comparative analysis of gender roles in selected works of fiction by Lília Momplé and Paulina Chiziane of Mozambique and Ana Paula Tavares of Angola with a specific focus on the representation of men and the ideas of masculinity. They draw on numerous aspects of postcolonial, feminist, and gender theories to examine concepts such as the patriarchal male, representations of the male body and sexuality, behavior, and relationships with the hopes of concluding how female Lusophone writers engage manliness, the male body, and gender roles.

Chapter four marks the transition to Afro-Lusophone films. Joseph Levi examines post-colonial identities in the cinema of Guinea-Bissau and São Tomé & Príncipe. He argues that the cinema of Lusophone Africa has not been a major focus among the academic community. Despite many financial and technical challenges, he shows how African directors and ones from Europe living in Lusophone Africa manage to convey the very essence of life in Guinea-Bissau and São Tomé & Príncipe and provide audiences insights on how to view and interpret the postcolonial identity in these two nations. in chapter five, Daniel da Silva also explores the cinema of São Tomé & Príncipe. In his chapter, he provides a brief overview of colonial and postcolonial film production in the island nation until 2000. Then, he examines how subsequent generations of filmmakers, harnessing different modes of dissemination and consumption, have radically revised the imagery of exoticism and essentialization that characterized colonial film and much of postcolonial production circuited to metropolitan consumption.

In chapter six, Patricia Ferreira explores the representation of orphans and the ways in which they either succumb to their social and political environment or have to adapt to it in two Lusophone films *Hollow City* (2004) by Maria João Ganga and *República di Mininus* (2012) by Flora Gomes which, with a contrasting approach, highlight a trajectory of loss and a trajectory of redemption. Ganga portrays Luanda as an urban space, derived from the emptiness of societal values and the lack of good role models, and contrasts it with Gomes's optimistic reinvention of society. She argues that the destruction and emptiness portrayed in *Republica de Mininus* are seen as inevitable to a much-desired rebirth of postcolonial African societies. Through this comparative analysis, she argues that Gomes' utopian project is rooted in a positive view of orphanhood, whereas Ganga's defeatist project conceives of the state of being an orphan as fatal.

The final chapter in this volume explores the relationship between text and film. My analysis explores the Cabo Verdean novel *O Testamento do Senhor*

Napumoceno da Silva Araújo by Germano Almeida and the film adaptation directed by Francisco Manso. The goal of this chapter is not to propose a new way in which scholars can examine a source text and its film adaptation; rather, drawing on Robert Stam's ideas of intertextuality, I examine what one can learn about a literary text based on its film adaptation. In my analysis, issues such as race, gender, and sexuality are explored along with aspects of film production, such as how making a co-produced film can impact the way the source text is portrayed on screen.

Together, these chapters demonstrate the literary and film production coming out of Hispanic and Lusophone Africa. Given advances in technology that have made it easier to publish texts and stream films online, the cultural production in these nations will likely flourish in years to come. The aim of this book is to contribute to the scholarship of these nations that have been overlooked by the academic community to varying degrees. In doing so, a wider audience can appreciate and gain new perspectives on the texts and films featured here.

Chapter 1

Trapped in the Closet: Complicity as Resistance in Donato Ndongo-Bidyogo's *Los poderes de la tempestad* (1997)

Sarita Naa Akuye Addy

Canadian Center for Diversity and Inclusion

Abstract

Donato Ndongo-Bidyogo's *Los poderes de la tempestad* (1997) is one of the most studied narratives about Equatorial Guinea. Its relativity to a wide readership hinges on its candid criticism of the colonial and postcolonial systems of oppression. The novel's evocation of resistance against the authoritarianism of the Nguemist regime also encompasses what resistance meant to the allies of the dictator. In this chapter, I discuss the controversial character, Ada, a female paramilitary officer who is complicit with the dictator. I argue that her alliance with the dictator within the social and political degeneration of Nguema's Equatorial Guinea is a kind of resistance against neo-colonialism and traditional Fang patriarchy. While the novel frames her resistance as anti-colonial, anti-patriarchal sentiments are revealed that point to a double oppression from both Nguemist and colonialist ideologies of the Guinean woman.

Keywords: Donato Ndongo-Bidyogo, *Los poderes de la tempestad*, Equatorial Guinea, Francisco Nguema

* * *

After independence from European colonialism, authoritarian rule has been a recurring *topos* in contemporary African novels that depict the 1970s. As many of these novels have shown, these dictatorships have proven to undermine the decolonizing agendas of many African countries. They have generally come to symbolize the consequences of overvaluing independence by placing utopian expectations on new governments. In addition to their brutally suppressive style of ruling, dictatorships and their language of violence expose the ideological limitations of nationalist movements in responding to the needs of their newly formed countries. Like the nationalisms that preceded them, dictatorships are conceptualized as masculine and respond mainly to the aspirations of the disenfranchised male figure post-independence. The exponential critic of the Equatorial Guinean narrative, Joseph Otabela (2004), observes that within the dictatorship novel of the seventies, there is a hypersexuality associated with the figure of the dictator, and this trait is emblematic of his absolute power and control over both public and private affairs (35). This de facto association of authoritarianism with power and sexuality provokes a gendered inquiry into questions of feminine subjectivity, compliance, and resistance under this system of governance. Donato Ndongo-Bidyogo's novel, *Los poderes de la tempestad*,[1] is panoramic in its exposé of life in Equatorial Guinea under its first president and dictator, Macías Nguema.[2] While it exposes the continuities of the systems of oppression and emits a discourse of resistance against the legacies of Spanish colonialism and the Nguema regime, it also shows what resistance means to those complicit with the dictator.

My reading of this text focuses on the character Ada, the female paramilitary officer who represents the dictator, Macías Nguema, within the novel.[3] Ada's position as a high-ranking officer and Nguema's ally is a catalyst for critically examining the interlocking nature of female political and cultural resistance. Her presence transmits the virulent and violent ethnocentric nationalism that the Nguema regime imposed nationwide to erase the Spanish cultural colonial legacy. She rejects the metaphoric and symbolic feminine roles within the discourse of nationalism as the biological reproducers of the nation and the transmitters of national culture in order to usurp the hypersexuality associated with dictators. This compels a critical inquiry into the avenues available to women to resist the gendered colonial and traditional cultural expectations

---

[1] *Los poderes de la tempestad,* published in 1997 is the second installment in the trilogy, *Los hijos de la tribu.* It is the sequel to Donato Ndongo- Bidyogo's first novel, *Las tinieblas de tu memoria negra* (1987).

[2] Francisco Macías Nguema was the first elected president of Equatorial Guinea after Spanish colonialism. From 1968 to 1979, Guinea was thrown into a violent and sanguinary dictatorship. Critics widely refer to his dictatorship *Nguemism*, a particular brand of authoritarianism in which he and his close allies arbitrarily governed the country. His administration was also characterized by the silencing and exile of intellectuals, incarcerations, and mass killings. The Swiss historian, Max Liniger-Goumaz (1988) estimates that approximately 125,000 citizens, which was about a quarter of the country's population, went into exile in neighbouring African countries and in Spain (56).

[3] Several arguments within the discussion in this chapter has been modified from a doctoral thesis.

placed on them and to escape institutionalized abuse. This discussion focuses on how her gender, social disenfranchisement due to colonialism, and her sexuality all interact in her complicity with the Nguemist regime. I argue that this alliance is enacted in a spirit of resistance against a perceived Western neo-colonial encroachment and Fang patriarchy. While her gender, sexuality, and complicity with the Nguema regime seemingly merge to articulate opposing discourses of resistance that may seem misaligned, they in effect display the complicated nature of political and cultural resistance for the postcolonial Guinean woman confined within the Nguema regime. While her alliance with the dictatorship enables her to resist Spanish colonialism politically, it simultaneously offers her a modicum of power through which she can escape institutionalized gendered abuse and experiment with same-sex desire, a concept that Fang traditional values stridently oppose.

Los poderes de la tempestad uses Ada to critique the economic and social violence of the colonial enterprise in Equatorial Guinea. However, as her exchanges with the protagonist indicate, acknowledging the cultural basis of colonial power does not erase the violence of conquest and control, especially on its female subject. In this regard, feminist thinkers have found postcolonial theory's focus on the male subject particularly negligent of how colonialism is itself a gendered paradigm of subjectivities. Like postcolonial theory, postcolonial feminism is grounded in, among other things, a practice of contesting the hegemonies of knowledge, power relations and challenging binaries rooted within colonialism. Although some critics consider it an approach more than a unified body of theory, postcolonial feminism evaluates representations of the female subaltern within imperial and nationalist historiography. Subsequently, it interrogates the gendered implications of the European colonial enterprise in regions that were formerly colonized. It also highlights the significance of gender in understanding colonialism and nationalism. Thus, this approach spotlights female subjectivities emanating from the colonial experience, especially class, ethnic, and religious oppression, which have marginalized women in contemporary postcolonial societies (Narayan 2009, 655).

Deconstructing the imposition of powerful political constructions of female subjectivities, especially within a postcolonial context, runs the risk of obscuring the traditional patriarchal systems operative before the advent of European colonialism. The postcolonial world was not a tabula rasa onto which colonizers uniquely inscribed their aspirations of conquest and domination. Here, Gayatri Spivak's intervention on the female colonial subject's social position in her essay "Can the Subaltern speak?" (1988) helps us understand how traditional patriarchy and its modern colonial variant form interlocking systems of erasure, which diminish the possibilities of hearing the female subaltern within Indian histories. Spivak calls attention to the historical and ideological factors through which representation of subaltern groups is mediated, highlighting the role of class in questions of sexual difference and gender. In a similar vein, the advent of nationalism recast the woman as a central figure within its rhetoric. However, it denied her power or direct access to that power. Anne McClintock (1995) has argued that nationalism is constructed as a gendered discourse and cannot be understood without a theory of gender power. For her, all nationalisms in their very inception are gendered because they spring from a masculinized perspective and conceptualization of the nation historically and socially. In this regard, the nation's needs are identified with the frustrations and aspirations of its men, and representations of national power and access to it depend on the prior construction of gender difference (353-55). As such, gender is essential to understanding Ada's alliance with Nguemism, a variant of nationalism erected on ethnocentric and anti-neo-colonialist ideologies. To properly contextualize Ada's opposition to the lawyer and his ideological stance within *Los poderes de la tempestad,* a careful study of Ada's complicity demands an inquiry into the historical conditions that condition her resistance.

Los poderes de la tempestad recounts the experiences of a biracial family, an unnamed Guinean lawyer and his Spanish wife, Ángeles, and their daughter, Rut, who return to Equatorial Guinea after an extended stay in the former metropolis, Madrid. To his utter dismay, he finds the country steeped in a violent dictatorship, even as it was on the brink of devastation, economically and socially. Together with his new family, this protagonist is thrown into an atmosphere conditioned by a violent Africanization campaign to erase Spanish culture within the national community.[4] In this asphyxiating socio-political environment, the text interrogates the ideologies of resistance by underlining the limitations of the reductionist and superficial anti-imperialist discourse

---

[4] Independence from Spain did not translate as freedom for Guinean citizens and Nguema's leadership failed to address Guinea's social and political problems. His government set off an economic, social, and political decline of the country. Within six months of independence, the president severed all diplomatic ties with Spain and pushed to align with the soviet communist bloc and its satellites. Nguema's regime, its lack of strategy for development and its nepotism, the deprivation of personal and political freedoms, coupled with extremely inefficient management and arbitrary incarcerations and mass killings drove many citizens to flee the country. His Africanization campaign attacked organized religions such as Christianity. Nguema denounced Christianity as alien to Africans and banned the use of Christian names. In November 1974 and again in April 1975, he banned all religious activities; sermons, meetings, funerals, and closed all churches (Decalo 1997, 80).

that the Nguema regime has embraced.[5] In his interactions with the regime's agents, he meets Ada, a high-ranking paramilitary officer who occasionally taunts him. While incarcerated, Ada attempts to rape the lawyer, and he rejects her advances. *Los poderes de la tempestad* demonstrates that the simplistic oppositional model of resistance does no more than reinforce colonial power dynamics and reduces the individual's identity solely to the anti-colonial struggle. The narrator constructs the colonial experience differently from the oppositional discourse and stresses that effective resistance demands the transformation of the colonized subject.

Even though the dictator never makes an appearance in the novel, the impact of his ideologies is visible within all aspects of national and private life. In this novel, it is Ada, the female paramilitary officer, who embodies the dictator. This transposition is interesting because Ndongo-Bidyogo's works seldom address gendered representations. Women are frequently the most affected by dictatorships, and in addition to the oppressions rooted in indigenous patriarchal traditions and European colonial norms that they suffer, dictatorships objectify, marginalize, and disempower them even more with the sole purpose of demonstrating the despot's absolute power in all national affairs (Otabela 2004, 35). The lawyer's few encounters with Ada enable us to see how her gender is essential to understanding her complicity with the Nguema regime.

Under Nguema, Guinean women were extremely vulnerable and easily became victims of institutionalized abuse and sexual violence.[6] Rather than being victimized and brutalized, Ada's complicity with Macías Nguema

---

[5] Nguema relied on a clan hegemony more than on an anti-colonialist ideology to govern. Although his leadership ideologies are not clearly defined, he exploited some communist practices to his benefit (Negrín-Fajardo 2017, 484-486). His alliance with the satellites of the communist bloc such as Cuba, North Korea, and China enabled him to appropriate some characteristics of communist leadership such as authoritarianism, and a cult of personality developed around the leader. Political observers have referred to him as the "Caligula" of Africa who failed to create a government relevant to Guinea's problems (Decalo 1997, 54; Baynham 1980, 69).

[6] According to Simon Baynham (1980), "Slave labour was also a hallmark of Macías' despotic regime. Macías forced girls, aged between 14 and 20, to work without pay on his private farm and coffee plantations in his native district of Mongomo. Many of them were made to submit to African and Cuban members of the presidential guard and the local militia. The use of young girls as forced labour was not new: in 1975, the President had ordered his troops to round up able-bodied young women and take them to Fernando Poo to harvest the cocoa crop. Whole families had at that time escaped across the frontier to Gabon and Cameroon to save their daughters from exploitation and degrading sexual abuse" (69).

required a usurpation of traits associated with masculinity, which insulated her from this gendered abuse. However, in doing so, Ada's actions within this role contradict the normative sexual behavior prescribed for women in Guinean society. Secondly, by aligning herself with Macías Nguema, Ada is fighting against neo-colonialist encroachment. This stance also demands an understanding of how colonialism's interaction with the cultural norms of the various communities of Spanish Guinea impacted women's lives, including their sexual expressions.

Traditional Patriarchy and Colonialism

At the onset of colonialism in sub-Saharan Africa, Spain propagated the religious discourse of Hispanidad, through which it meant to bring civilization and enlightenment to the territories of Spanish Guinea.[7] This justification for colonizing made missionaries the primary agents of this imperial project. In the territories of Spanish Guinea, the Spanish colonists faced strong kinship structures that they felt they had to break if they were to successfully "civilize" the natives (Tofiño-Quesada 2003, 144). In light of this, Spain's interference in these communities' cultures was done to fulfill its humanitarian task of assisting its African subjects' physical and moral upliftment (Stucki 2019, 9). However, this justification was alimented by the image of the helpless woman, suppressed by native customs, and whose predicament necessitated an agenda to "uplift" African women in its colonies by educating them on European norms culture. This discourse essentially "feminized" Iberian colonialism to reflect the humanitarianism within the imperial project (Stucki 2019, 12).

Despite this orientalist view, there were aspects of native customs that Guinean women had to resist if they were to escape traditional patriarchal oppression. Before Catholicism, Guinean women faced various injustices rooted in patriarchal norms, and these women responded by using indigenous strategies to mitigate oppression (Allan 2019, 66). In his analysis of *Ekomo* (1985), written by María Nsué Angüe, Hubert Edzodzomo Ondo points out that traditionally, the role of the Fang woman was strictly confined to realms of reproduction, domesticity, and rendering economic support to their spouses, thereby excluding them from making decisions that affect them personally (2013, 97). Nnanga, the female protagonist in *Ekomo*, laments her invisibility within the social programming of her community: "Yo no soy más que un perfil recortado contra el contorno que me rodea, que es el de la selva. Mi presencia,

---

[7] When the Spanish Crown took possession of the islands and mainland region which make up Equatorial Guinea in 1844, it rechristened its sub-Saharan colony "Los territorios españoles del Golfo de Guinea," until independence in October 1968 when it was changed to Equatorial Guinea.

poco advertida, no es sino una presencia-ausencia cuya importancia nada tiene que ver con el proceso normal de los acontecimientos. Vivo y respiro con la conciencia de mi propia impotencia" (1985, 23).

The marginalization of women within Guinean ethnicities does not also imply the absence of structures within their native cultures through which women could counter repression. For instance, among the Fang, *Bwiti* religious practices provided spaces for women to challenge gendered systems of power. There were all-female institutions, such as the *Mewungo*, which were feared by men (Allan 2019, 68). This sect dealt with problems women faced, such as infertility, negligence of husbandly duties, and child mortality. Before Christianity, Bubi women could hold important positions through which they influenced decisions, such as which male leader was chosen, which marriages were dissolved, and what punishments to mete out to those who violated the community's norms (Allan 2019, 76).

The impact of Christianity and Spanish legal administration on Guinean women's lives are varied, complex and not at all universal. As Enrique Okenve (2007) notes, conversion to Christianity allowed some women to take on more significant roles within their communities' religious activities. While some women knew how to use Christianity to gain more rights and expand their sphere of influence, other aspects of their rights were eroded (126). The imposition of Catholicism impacted women's sexual freedoms, especially for Fang women. Unlike other Guinean ethnicities, Fang women were allowed to explore their sexualities before they were married. Conversion to Catholicism among the Fang "converted female sexuality into a terrible and dangerous force to be tamed in and outside of marriage" (Allan 2019, 70). Whereas Christian missionaries sometimes gave sanctuary to women who fled abusive spouses, the dissolution of marriage under Catholicism was even more difficult.

The feminization of the colonial discourse did not insulate native women from sexual abuse, exploitation, or European gender norms. These norms existed primarily to preserve the empire and stabilize afro-Iberian identities. Gustau Nerín (1998) argues in *Historia en blanco y negro* that the hypersexualization of Spanish men during colonialism served to trivialize the sexual exploitation of the native women by white men. Institutions like the *Patronato de Indígenas* failed to protect indigenous women from the sexual exploitation of white men, especially those who did not have the status of being emancipated.[8] This body enforced controversial and discriminatory laws that,

---

[8] In 1928, Spain implemented the *Patronato de Indígenas* Act in this colony. This served to regulate civil rights status, economic prospects and social mobility of the Africans who

in addition to enforcing Spanish morality and cultural hegemony, institutionalized the patriarchal norms that ensured their abuse (Allan 2019, 72-4).

The change in government in the Iberian Peninsula in 1939 did not ease the overall impact of marginalization that indigenous women faced emanating from patriarchy and the racism and sexism inherent within colonialism. Under the Falange, Spain authorities used discourses of gender to further their imperial projects. After the provincialization of the territories of Spanish Guinea, the Falange sent its women's section, known as the *Sección Femenina*, to their African colonies to indoctrinate the indigenous populations with its own version of gender roles. Until independence, the *Sección Femenina* partnered mainly with local Guinean religious organizations and the Catholic church to reinforce gendered practices that revolved primarily around domesticity and preserving Spanish cultural hegemony within the colony (Villena and Cerdeño 2014, 126-28).

While staging its economic and industrial exploitation, Spain's colonialism of Spanish Guinea also impacted Guinean women's lives in highly complex ways. Under colonialism, Guinean women had to resist racism, sexism, and classism. These barriers incited various responses from the women, some of whom either gained few rights or whose social privileges were eroded, diminished, or altogether lost. However, despite the diverse nature of pre-colonial Fang, Ndowé, Bubi, Fernandino and Annobonese cultures, Spanish colonialism in Equatorial Guinean institutionalized patriarchal norms.

Challenging Colonialism and Normative Female Sexual Behavior

Ada's utterances in *Los poderes de la tempestad* shows that independence from Spain did not overturn the institutionalized marginalization —within Fang culture and under colonial administration— that Guinean women suffered. Neither did the new state address structural changes on women's rights, and their abuse was prevalent at the domestic and institutional levels. For instance, the lawyer's cousin, Avomo, is often beaten by her husband. The military officers verbally insult Ángeles and subject her to humiliating physical

---

found themselves living within Spanish territories. Ndongo- Bidyogo describes this Act as: "una institución de carácter público con personalidad propia y capacidad para adquirir, poseer y enajenar bienes de todas clases, encargada de coadyuvar a la acción colonizadora del Estado, procurando el fomento, desarrollo y defensa de los intereses morales y materiales de los indígenas que no pueden valerse por sí mismos." This form of social control subverted the local social hierarchies within the indigenous societies. Under this Act, it accorded "emancipado pleno," "emancipado parcial," and "no emancipado" statuses to their African subjects (1977, 55).

punishments in all the couple's encounters with the authorities. Under Nguema's dictatorship, both Guinean and Spanish women continue to be victims of patriarchal brutalities. Unlike the other women in the novel, Ada is not a victim of the regime but one of its allies, an unusual situation that accords her power usually reserved for men. She expresses this power predominantly through sex. This connection between sexuality and power is a patriarchal trope that predates colonialism itself, but which was reinforced during the colonial times. The feminization of colonial spaces, coupled with the white male colonizer's hypersexualization, served to justify European economic and even sexual exploitation of the most vulnerable native population.

Michel Cornaton (1990) explains this relationship between sex and power : "Le pouvoir et la sexualité son deux réalités intriquées: Comment le pouvoir pourrait-il se reproduire, si ce n'était pas sexuellement? Là où il y a production et reproduction est le sexe, fût-il imaginaire, ainsi que le fait apparaître la psychanalyse. Le pouvoir est aussi un lieu de plaisir et la sexualité le domain du pouvoir sur l'autre et sur soi-même" (40). Cornaton identifies the sex act as a site where power is reproduced and exercised over the dominated, while the very act asserts the dominant one's power over himself. The exercise of power also becomes a location of pleasure. Ada's actions in this domain is representative of the hypersexuality associated with dictators. She tries to take the place of Ángeles' husband, by usurping the role of the man in the sexual act, and then later, demanding sex from the lawyer while he was in Blavis prison (1997, 66). She exercises this power predominantly through unsolicited sexual advances, sexual innuendos, and the sexual act itself (1997, 40-1; 257-9). Her engagement in the sexual act then becomes a site for reproducing and reclaiming the autonomy that the Guinean had lost as a result of Spanish colonization. Even after independence, Guineans still had to deal with the general inequalities which was caused by colonialism prevalent within the country. Clearly for Ada, Spanish colonial exploitation lay at the root of Guinea's national problems:

> ¿Qué han hecho por ti? ¿Qué han hecho por tu pueblo? Sólo explotarnos y llevarse nuestras riquezas, para enriquecerse a costa nuestra. Sólo somos los hombros sobre los que se aúpan para alcanzar su cielo, su bienestar, egoístamente, y ya es hora de que rompamos eso, porque estamos hartos de soportar su peso. Y tú debes decidir de que parte estás. (257-258)

Ada's exertion of power through sex is significant in this novel because non-hetero female sexuality is rarely discussed in the Guinean novel. Apart from Trifonia Melibea Obono's *La bastarda* (2016), which explores female homosexuality within contemporary Guinean society, questions of "non-normative" female sexual behaviour within the post-independence novel remain mostly unexplored. Joanna Boampong (2015) observes that lesbianism within African literature does not receive much attention because many of the continent's scholars still consider it non-African. She indicates that perhaps the author, Donato Ndongo-Bidyogo, seems to draw attention to this erroneous notion (65-6). As *Los poderes de la tempestad* shows, Ada has lesbian inclinations and manifests sexual desires that are contrary to those prescribed by African tradition. However, her complicity with the regime positions her within what Homi Bhabha refers to as a "liminal space" where she can fulfill these desires. Within the novel, these spaces are hidden crevices marked by the absence of the panopticon, a situation that allows for slippages and deviance from the expected social norms. Areas such as the strip search room and the prison cell where potential subversives are interrogated are entry and exit points into and out of her socio-cultural environment. Hence, Ada's position within the administration provides the perfect opportunity to manifest her resistance to the heterosexuality imposed on the Fang woman.

Within a patriarchal society that constrains the woman into a domestic and childbearing role, Ada transgresses the norm by being a woman who seeks her own sexual gratification with either sex, isolated from its childbearing function. In contrast to the other women, she is portrayed as a woman who refuses to be the object of male pleasure. Ángeles' recollection of her encounter with Ada, when the latter performed a strip search on her, reveals that Ada is conscious of the sexual expectations placed on women (41). However, instead of complying, she defies these gendered norms by using the protagonist and his wife as objects of pleasure. When Ada confronts the lawyer in prison, she unleashes her pent-up feelings: "Ahora te tengo a mi disposición, para mí sola, abogado. Puedo hacer contigo lo que me plazca sin que tenga que dar cuenta a nadie" (259). As opposed to her earlier observation of the traditional expectations placed on women to sexually please men, Ada's emphasis on her pleasure marks a break from being an object to being a subject of her sexual gratification.

With her successful usurpation of masculine privilege, as the unquestionable partner whose demand for pleasure must be satisfied, Ada demands the lawyer's compliance in the same way that Guinean society demands it of women. In acting this way, Ada resists both colonial and traditional patriarchal ideals of normative female sexual behaviour. Her complicity with a regime that brutalizes her kind speaks to the paucity of avenues available to the Guinean woman to contest the normative heterosexuality prescribed for them.

The Guinean woman's marginalization under the Nguema regime worsened. Women were easy targets for forced recruitments for work on the cocoa plantations of the dictator and were also vulnerable to the sexual exploitation of Nguema's soldiers. The protagonist's father complains: "sólo quiere nuestro café y cacao y nuestras mujeres y nuestras hijas, que son obligadas a ir a cultivar las fincas de cacahuetes y de plátanos y de yuca y de ñames en Mongomo, donde encima las usan como quieren y nos las devuelven embarazadas y ya no nos hacen caso, así destruyen nuestras familias, hijo" (197). Even though Ada enjoys the power and privilege of her status, she is still conscious of how her gender makes her an easy victim under this regime. Ángeles recounts to her husband: "Y al final me dijo que yo era sólo una mujer como todas, como ella misma, que os creéis las blancas si todas tenemos lo mismo en el mismo sitio y sólo servimos para el placer de los hombres" (41). Here, Ada's words corroborate women's vulnerability both within the colonial Spanish and the postcolonial Guinean social systems as a kind of oppression that cuts across race. It is perhaps the futility of this situation that propels her complicity with a regime which positions her to usurp the power traditionally accorded to men. By aligning with the Nguema regime as one of its agents, she insulates herself and acquires immunity against the gendered violence which the regimes operations used as a form of control.

Rose Weitz (2010) in "A History of Women's Bodies" reminds us that "Only by looking at the embodied experiences of women, as well as how those experiences are socially constructed, can we fully understand women's lives, women's position in society, and the possibilities for resistance against that position" (11). Similarly, only by scrutinizing the hypersexuality of the dictator incarnate can we begin to grasp the extremely limited avenues of resistance available to women and why Ada must appropriate this attribute as a vehicle for venting her sexual frustration. In effect, she borrows the same tools of the patriarchy, which have been used to silence her to resist the colonialist and patriarchal constrictions on the Guinean woman. Although they allow her to temporarily "beat him at his own game" (Lorde 2007, 2), they never enable Ada to bring about genuine change. In other words, her ability to act upon her desires only within this capacity reinforces the unacceptability of such practices within the broader context of Guinean society.

Ada's unsolicited and flirtatious behavior, coupled with her sexual innuendos, makes the narrator view her constantly with suspicion. By virtue of her behavior, she stands outside of the definition of an acceptable Fang woman. Furthermore, her desires are misaligned with the national development project that the protagonist, who embodies the nation, holds for the country. Ada, then, is a complex character onto whom the narrator inscribes the failed resistance of the Guinean state. The Nguemist regime's simplistic inversion of this hierarchy, as the novel proves, does not constitute effective resistance but rather perpetuates the same forms of oppressions that independence ought to abolish. As proof of this, the lawyer vomits, metaphoric of his rejection of Ada, and by extension, the dictator's grotesque actions and ideologies meant to recondition him. The compendium of Ada's speeches and actions characterizes her as an agent for the state, as a spokesperson for the dictator. Although she talks, her lectures consist of orders, monologues, and questions that no one answers, further reinforcing the puppeteering role that she plays within the government. Overall, she has no real power of her own and cannot affect any change for herself as a woman. Nevertheless, her usurpation of this role makes her visible and registers her protest against an interlocking system of oppression that silences her kind.

Ada's complicity with the Nguemist regime is a paradox in itself. On the one hand, she is repressed and, on the other, a repressor herself. Her visibility within the newly minted nation and access to power hinges on the usurpation of traits and privileges reserved for the male citizen. She is complicit with a regime that rejects her sexual orientation as unAfrican and embodies a hypersexuality that enables her to fulfill her same-sex desires, even when it somewhat erodes her agency as a Fang woman. Thus, her resistance as a woman and a Guinean citizen is enacted within a complex nexus of dictatorship, patriarchy, and colonialism, and her actions speak to the paucity of avenues for resistance available to women who lived under Nguema's government. Even though she wields a modicum of power, she can still not affect any structural change that can truly validate her sexuality and liberate herself. Furthermore, this character espouses a nationalist rhetoric that constantly rehashes a colonial history that brutally exploited the nation. However, in the same breath, she exposes Nguemism's limitation as an ideology that perpetually locks its adherents in a constant battle of opposition against anything Western. In essence, Ada is trapped within the same Manichean binaries imposed by colonialism; nevertheless, it instigates her complicity with a system that erases her agency. Ada thus becomes the metaphor of a failed resistance, a purely oppositional model to the European cultural legacy that appropriates colonial power and merely inverts its social paradigms.

As Anne McClintock (1995) has observed, preliminary analyses of anti-colonial nationalisms have tended to ignore how this movement is connected to issues relating to women's full civic participation. This calls for a feminist theory of nationalism, which will, among other things, be vested in "bringing into historical visibility women's active cultural and political participation in national formations" (357). Similarly, *Los poderes de la tempestad* signals the need for an inquiry into the social histories of Equatorial Guinean women who lived under Macías Nguema. This exposé also beckons an inquiry into Guinean women's roles and positionality within the nguemist discourse of nationhood.

Works Cited

Allan, Joanna. *Silenced Resistance: Women, Dictatorships, and Genderwashing in Western Sahara and Equatorial Guinea*. Madison WI: University of Wisconsin Press, 2019.

Baynham, Simon. "Equatorial Guinea: The Terror and the Coup." *World Today* 36 (2): 65–71, 1980.

Boampong, Joanna. "La miliciana Ada y la dinámica de poder en la literatura africana hispanófona." *EPOS: Revista de Filología* XXXI: 61-70, 2015.

Cornaton, Michel. *Pouvoir Et Sexualité Dans Le Roman Africain: Analyse Du Roman Africain Contemporain*. Paris: L'Harmattan, 1990.

Decalo, Samuel. *Psychoses of Power: African Personal Dictatorships*. Gainesville: Florida Academic Press, 1997.

Liniger-Goumaz, Max. *Small is not always Beautiful: The Story of Equatorial Guinea*. London: Hurst, 1988.

Lorde, Audre. "The Master's Tools Will Never Dismantle the Master's House." Sister Outsider: Essays and Speeches, 110-114. Berkeley, CA: Crossing Press, 2007.

Morales Villena, Amalia, and Vieitez Cerdeño, Soledad. "La Sección Femenina en la 'llamada de África': Saharauis y guineanas en el declive del colonialismo español," *Vegueta. Anuario de la Facultad de Geografía e Historia* 14: 117-133, 2014.

McClintock, Anne. "No longer in a future heaven: Nationalism, Gender and Race" in *Imperial Leather: Race, Gender, and Sexuality in the Colonial Conquest*, 352-389, New York: Routledge, 1995.

Narayan, Anjana. "Postcolonial/Subaltern Feminism." In *Encyclopedia of Gender and Society*, edited by Jodi O'Brien, 654–59. Thousand Oaks: Sage Publications, 2009.

Nerín, Gustau. *Guinea Ecuatorial, historia en blanco y negro*. Barcelona: Península, 1998.

Negrín-Fajardo, Olegario. "Una Singular 'Educación Cívica' para Guinea Ecuatorial: las sentencias doctrinales de la dictadura de Francisco Macías Nguema (1968-1979)." In *Conversaciones con un Maestro (Liber Amicorum)*, 481-491. Madrid: Ediciones Académicas, 2017.

Ndongo-Bidyogo, Donato. *Las tinieblas de tu memoria negra*. Madrid: Editorial Fundamentos, 1987.

___. *Los poderes de la tempestad*. Madrid: Morandi, 1997.

Nsué Angüe, María, J. R. García, and Gloria Nistal. *Ekomo*. Madrid: Sial Ediciones, 2007.

Obono, Trifonia Melibea. *La bastarda*. Madrid: Editorial Flores Raras, 2016.

Okenve, Enrique. *Equatorial Guinea 1927-1979: A New African Tradition*. London: University of London Press, 2007.

Ondo, Hubert Edzodzomo. Les représentations de la femme dans *Ekomo* (1985) de María Nsué Angüe et *Hija de la Fortuna* (1998) de Isabel Allende. University of Tours, PhD dissertation, 2013.

Otabela Mewolo, Joseph Désiré. "La figura del dictador: Macías Nguema y Rafael Trujillo en *Los poderes de la tempestad* de Donato Ndongo-Bidyogo y en *La fiesta del chivo* de Mario Vargas Llosa." *ConNotas* II, (2): 27-46, 2004.

Spivak, Gayatri. "Can the Subaltern speak?" In *Marxism and the Interpretation of Culture,* edited by Cary Nelson and Lawrence Grossberg, 217-313. Urbana: University of Illinois Press, 1988.

Stucki, Andreas. *Violence and Gender in Africa's Iberian Colonies: Feminizing the Portuguese and Spanish Empire, 1950s–1970s.* Cham: Springer International Publishing, 2019.

Tofiño-Quesada, Ignacio. "Spanish Orientalism: Uses of the Past in Spain's Colonization in Africa." *Comparative Studies of South Asia, Africa and the Middle East* 23 (1-2), 141–48, 2003.

Weitz, Rose. "A History of Women's Bodies." In *The Politics of Women's Bodies: Sexuality, Appearance, and Behavior.* New York: Oxford University Press, 2019.

Chapter 2

Imagination and Reality in *Comissão das Lágrimas* by António Lobo Antunes

Paulo Rodrigues Ferreira

University of North Carolina at Chapel Hill

Abstract

Due to his experience as a military doctor in the Colonial War, António Lobo Antunes, one of the most celebrated Lusophone authors, wrote profusely about the collapse of the Portuguese Empire in Africa. Since his literary work as a whole may be seen as an interpretation of the contemporary history of Portugal, one of the aims of this article is precisely to evaluate how Lobo Antunes perceives topics such as colonialism and postcolonialism. One will also try to understand how direct experience affects the recounting of past events. Particularly relevant in this article will be the analysis of *Comissão das Lágrimas* (2011), a novel in which Lobo Antunes gives life to Cristina, a mentally challenged woman who digresses into her fragmented, traumatic past in Angola to give an account of the terrors perpetrated by her father, a member of the so-called Comissão das Lágrimas. Supposedly, this organization was created in 1977 to persecute and arrest the intellectuals involved in a failed coup to overthrow Agostinho Neto's government. Considering that writers such as Pepetela deny the existence of Comissão das Lágrimas, among the ambitions of this article is to examine how Lobo Antunes describes this complex period of Angolan history. Through literary techniques such as the stream of consciousness, the Portuguese author often dives into history to scrutinize the psychological dimensions of human existence. Consequently, one will try to answer the following questions: how do Lobo Antunes's literary techniques help him to recount historical events? How can fiction help readers to apprehend the complexities of history? What are the frontiers between reality and fiction in his oeuvre, especially in *Comissão das Lágrimas*?

Keywords: Stream of consciousness, Angola, Comissão das Lágrimas, Portugal, history, postcolonialism

* * *

Lobo Antunes and the collapse of the Portuguese Empire

António Lobo Antunes, one of the most distinguished and complex Lusophone authors, wrote profusely about the collapse of the Portuguese Empire in Africa. The fact that he served as a military doctor in the Colonial War (1961-1974)[1] helps to explain his interest in topics such as colonialism and postcolonialism. Decadence, degeneration, and corruption are keywords to absorb the literary works of someone who mastered the art of interpreting the Portuguese ways of life. Lobo Antunes envisions Portugal as a stagnated country that is unable to overcome chronic economic and political crises. Salazar's dictatorship appears in his fiction as an alienating regime that condemned millions of people to indigence and narrow-mindedness. Since the writer visualizes corruption and mediocrity as two predominant characteristics of Portuguese society, his novels illustrate the nation's inadequacy for democracy and in the face of demanding challenges arising from the urgency to find material progress and abundance.[2]

One of the aims of this article is precisely to understand how Lobo Antunes perceives the contemporary history of Portugal. Considering that Angola plays a tremendous role in his fiction, another ambition is to reflect upon topics that are meaningful to the author, such as the Portuguese presence in Africa. Due to his personal experience as a young doctor in the Colonial War, one will also try to evaluate how his subjective impressions affect the recounting of the past. Additionally, considering Lobo Antunes's propensity to explore human beings through narrative techniques such as the stream of consciousness, another goal of this article is to assess the worth of his incursions into history. *Comissão das Lágrimas*, a novel that focuses on a specific and controversial historical event, is going to be particularly important when answering the following question: What are the boundaries between fiction and reality in Lobo Antunes's oeuvre?

Lobo Antunes's novels centered around the Colonial War often combine the most intense bleakness with parody, satire, and other elements used with the intention of ridiculing and reevaluating history. By way of illustration, in *As Naus* (1988), one of his most celebrated works, Lobo Antunes satirizes the end

---

[1] António Lobo Antunes lived in Angola from 1971 to 1973.
[2] In an interview, he declared that Portugal deserves much better than being ruled by generations of mediocre politicians that don't even know how to speak proper Portuguese. António Lobo Antunes, "Não tenho muito jeito para viver", *Visão*, November 20, 2014, http://visao.sapo.pt/actualidade/cultura/antonio-lobo-antunes-nao-tenho-muito-jeito-para-viver=f802105.

of the war in Africa and the return of thousands of *retornados*.[3] He turns famous navigators like Pedro Álvares Cabral, Diogo Cão or Vasco da Gama, into twentieth-century ordinary men who deal with the loss of the remnants of a colonial Empire that has just come to an end, after five centuries of existence.[4] By contrasting a catastrophic present with a glorious past inhabited by discoverers, kings, and literary geniuses, Lobo Antunes deconstructs, quite comically, a supposedly irreprehensible historical legacy. After crossing the seas and discovering unknown lands, Vasco da Gama and other illustrious national figures face the inevitability of coming back to Portugal, a country that is far from being the once prosperous and cosmopolitan realm. In *As Naus*, these former heroes are vulgar citizens who have nothing in their pockets except desolation and penury.[5] Thus, the return of the explorers is a metaphor for the evanescence of heroism and grandeur. Even though the collapse of the imperial dream coincided with the end of *Estado Novo*'s dictatorship–and a possible future of prosperity and democracy–, Lobo Antunes seldom envisions optimistic prospects for his country: Portugal became a free, democratic nation, but all its past evils–corruption, decadence, mediocrity–remained unchanged. Besides the inability to overcome past problems, there is no economic growth, culture is nonexistent, scarcity is overwhelming, and Europe and modernity are always too far from Portugal to be palpable. To put it differently, in Lobo Antunes's fiction there is a constant assumption that not even the advent of democracy was able to solve Portugal's endemic difficulties.[6] That postulation drives the reader to ask: How can a country thrive or find prosperity when its inhabitants are stuck in immemorial times? In *As Naus*, the writer does not provide straight answers to this kind of question and implies that laughter and mockery are adequate instruments to describe the lives of people who are confronted not only with their physical and mental limitations, but with a nonsensical reality.

The setting of Lobo Antunes's novels is usually a specific moment in Portuguese history. However, far from being a mere chronicler of the

---

[3] Basically, *retornados* means: Portuguese living in the African colonies who were repatriated to Portugal after their independence in 1974-1975.

[4] Maria Alzira Seixo, *Os Romances de António Lobo Antunes, Análise, interpretação, resumos e guiões de leitura* (Lisbon: D. Quixote, 2002), 129.

[5] By caricaturing and relegating these historical figures to a subordinate position, the writer reexamines and questions history. He desacralizes the past and confronts it with his own reality to evaluate and accept the present state of things. Silvana M. Pessoa Oliveira, "Relendo as naus portuguesas–ironia e paródia na obra de Lobo Antunes," *SCRIPTA* 4, nº 8 (2001): 297.

[6] María Luisa Blanco, *Conversaciones con António Lobo Antunes* (Madrid: Ediciones Siruela, 2001), 51.

Portuguese disgraces, the writer distorts, deforms, and recounts historical events without following a chronological order. Through literary techniques for which he is famous, namely the so-called polyphonic narrative, in which he erects a multiple set of autonomous voices, Lobo Antunes blends a profusion of actions that occurred in the past with emotions that emerge in the present.[7] Chronicling historical events as they happened is less important for him than scrutinizing the psychological dimensions of existence: the past is a pretext to dissect the human psyche and what lies below the surface.[8] That is notorious, for example, in *Comissão das Lágrimas* (2011), a book where Lobo Antunes provides the reader with little information: besides knowing that the action takes place in 1977, one is aware of the existence of an organization – Comissão das Lágrimas – that tortures people in Angola, but it is perceptible that factual history plays a secondary role in his fiction. As Richard Zenith puts it, this author's novels may be used "to focus on Portugal's long and troubled relationship with Africa. To focus on it not from a political but from a psychological point of view."[9] Antunes's concern is less Angolan history than the representation of destruction and brutality in a place where happiness is a mere utopia. In the referred novel, Lobo Antunes narrates the story of a family that suffers the damaging effects of physical and mental barbarism, and the story of that family becomes the story of many other families. In other words, by depicting a specific character, Lobo Antunes depicts mankind. His characters are not only Portuguese or Angolan, but men and women that are worlds in miniature.

Unsurprisingly, Angola holds a privileged position in Lobo Antunes's fiction, and his topology of that country is both caricatural and nightmarish (Madureira 1995, 23). As mentioned before, in *As Naus* humor combines with the sternest melancholy. One of the characters, the poet Luís de Camões, comes home from Africa with a coffin containing his father. The tragicomic image of Camões returning to Portugal with his father's dead body symbolizes the decay of a civilization. The greatest national poet returns to his homeland carrying his deceased father – in this context, the father is nothing less than the image of a country that succumbed to self-inflicted injuries – but bureaucrats take an eternity to authorize him to bury the body (Conrad 2009). Bureaucrats represent mediocrity, the victory of banality over geniality. Lobo Antunes is

---

[7] Maria Alzira Seixo, "Still Facts and Living Fictions," in *Facts and Fictions of António Lobo Antunes*, ed. by Victor K. Mendes (Massachusetts: UMass Dartmouth, 2017), 19-44.

[8] Robert Humphrey, *Stream of Consciousness in the Modern Novel* (London: University of California Press, 1972), 4.

[9] Richard Zenith, "The geographer's manual: the place of place in António Lobo Antunes," in *Facts and Fictions of António Lobo Antunes*, 135.

telling his readers that the future of Portugal is oblivion and superficiality. The end of the African adventure brings freedom to Africans but dooms the Portuguese to a meaningless life. Needless to say, this absence of meaning pervades all his fiction.

Several other books by Lobo Antunes portray the eclipse of the Portuguese glory by giving the sense of a simultaneously frightening and pathetic reality. *Memória de Elefante* (1979), his first novel, and probably the simplest in terms of structure, describes the life of a young, divorced psychiatrist – Lobo Antunes's alter-ego – who has recently returned from the military service in Africa. In Lisbon, he struggles to adapt to a new reality but is unable to overcome misery and a fastidious daily routine. Obsessed with Africa, he deals with solitude, sadness, and disappointment, and tries to find comfort in the arms of prostitutes. Published in the same year, *Os Cus de Judas* explores the Portuguese oppression in Africa and the effects of war on an ex-combatant. Once again, Lobo Antunes seems to be more interested in submerging in the depths of human despair and existential terrors than in history per se. War destroys people, turns ex-soldiers into inept, misfit creatures for whom words like love or joy are forgotten dreams. Therefore, in his eyes, this is the legacy of colonialism, the burden that Portugal must bear.

In *Fado Alexandrino* (1985), his fifth book, Lobo Antunes inaugurates an innovative narrative style: a multiplicity of characters, or interwoven voices, replaces the author's first or third person. This type of narration, which one might call stream of consciousness,[10] connects a plurality of perspectives and points of view.[11] The aim is to create the impression that existence is not only complex and difficult to apprehend, but also that through all the fragments and whispers, there is a background voice – the writer's voice – that interprets and gives meaning and cohesion to the narrative. Consequently, Antunes places himself as the entity that ties this panoply of voices together.[12] At the core of *Fado Alexandrino* is the Colonial War, but this time the action takes place in Mozambique instead of Angola. As in other "African novels", Lobo Antunes

---

[10] Considering the fluidity of some literary techniques and narrative modes, one might also suggest that Vargas Llosa's "communicating vessels", a technique in which episodes that appear in different spaces and times are connected by a common denominator, may also help to understand how some Lobo Antunes's books are structured. Vargas Llosa, *Cartas a un joven novelista* (Madrid: Alfaguara, 2011), 128. See also Raymond Leslie Williams, *Mario Vargas Llosa: a life of writing* (Texas: Univ. of Texas, 2014).

[11] Bakhtin called this plurality a "multiplicity of independent and immiscible voices and consciences." M. Bakhtin, *Questões de literatura e de estética* (São Paulo: EDUNESC, 1990), 4.

[12] Felipe Cammaert, "You don't invent anything: memory and the patterns of fiction in Lobo Antunes's work," in *Facts and Fictions of António Lobo Antunes*, 279.

gives life to a man that goes to war against his will and is subjected to all kinds of mortifications. Also worthy of note is *O Esplendor de Portugal* (1997), a novel that deals with this recurring topic of war, or postwar, in Africa. Lobo Antunes puts in evidence the pointless destruction brought about by the military conflict. He also exposes the decrepitude of a fallen empire, the stupidity and lack of leadership of the Portuguese military, and the poverty and ugliness of innocent civilians that are unable to escape the massacres of war.

Salazar's regime is represented in these novels as a despotic system that locked away the well-being of millions of Portuguese. On the one hand, the writer points out that authoritarianism imprisoned and pulverized Portugal's future. On the other hand, Lobo Antunes indirectly criticizes his own people for their tendency to blindly obey without questioning themselves about the purpose of life. When considering Lobo Antunes's literary work, one concludes that the analysis of the Portuguese ways of being is at the top of his priorities. Hence, aside from debating the relevance of colonialism and postcolonialism[13] in his oeuvre, one might also ask questions that are only apparently secondary. For example, why does the author often describe his countrymen as narrow-minded and mediocre? Why is poverty omnipresent in his fiction? Why are his characters so averse to change? In other words, why do the Portuguese struggle so much to overcome provincialism? Like the philosophers José Gil and Eduardo Lourenço,[14] the writer meditates upon his country's decadence, reflects on the past and the future, and comes up with evidence that Salazar's regime almost destroyed a cultural legacy with centuries of history. Lobo Antunes goes further and seems to ask: Why isn't Portugal capable of overcoming past traumas and finding material progress? After the end of the Discoveries and numerous historical misfortunes, why is the country still drowning in chronic economic, cultural, and political crises? According to José Gil, who published *Portugal, Hoje: o Medo de Existir,* a book that became a bestseller and was widely discussed in Portugal, several decades of dictatorship imposed a fear of existing upon the Portuguese. By fear of existing, he means a fear of cultivating self-esteem, a fear of being European, a fear of confronting the challenges brought about by modern life (Gil, 2004). Even though there is no direct connection between Gil and Lobo Antunes's works, it is impossible to analyze the novelist's fiction without invoking this fear that permeates most of his characters, inhabitants of a world composed of repression, rage, isolation, mental imbalance and psychiatric disorders. It is as if Antunes were applying

---

[13] And topics such as identity, violence, and war.
[14] See, for example, *O Labirinto da Saudade* (1972), by E. Lourenço, or *O Medo de Existir* (2004), by J. Gil.

the techniques of psychotherapy not only to people but to his own country (Arnaut 2011, 78).

Since Lobo Antunes's abovementioned novels have certain elements in common – Africa, solitude, retornados, depression, despair – they are vital to understanding *Comissão das Lágrimas*. Recurrently in these books, the writer depicts a soldier or a retornado's journey into the futile world of Lisbon, capital of a country that only offers scarcity, tears, shadows, and memories of a past that is more impactful and tangible than the present. In Esplendor de Portugal, for instance, the reader follows the expectations and failures of three different generations of colonizers who share feelings of abandonment, guilt, and loss. There is another aspect that connects these characters: racism. In fact, Lobo Antunes often portrays colonizers as racists who humiliate Africans. To put it differently, Africans don't exist or aren't important in a narrative that primarily focuses on the existential conflicts of white men and women. Lobo Antunes doesn't write from the perspective of an African (Gould 2017, 159). Possibly, the writer's lack of concern for Africans comes from the observation of other soldiers' behaviors during his stay in Angola. Furthermore, by putting this racism in evidence, Lobo Antunes highlights the lack of proximity between two separate worlds. When reading his novels, one invariably gets the impression that colonizers talk about Africans with disdain and repugnance: Africans are not worthy of making love with white women, they lack the necessary politeness to share a meal with colonizers, they don't have enough civility, education or social condition to wear the clothes of a European. Lobo Antunes explores these racial prejudices not only to emphasize the brutality and ignorance of a specific group of soldiers or colonizers, but to characterize the absurdity of all that surrounded colonialism.

Comissão das Lágrimas: a journey into darkness

To examine Lobo Antunes's fiction and contextualize it with the contemporary history of Portugal, one must be careful not to give factual value to what likely is a product of the imagination (Moutinho 2017, 72). That is particularly true when commenting on a novel that describes a controversial historical event. One of the ambitions of this article is to examine how Lobo Antunes recreates a historical occurrence whose existence is still dubious nowadays. Comissão das Lágrimas is the name of the secret organization that arrested the suspects of a conspiracy to overthrow the government of Agostinho Neto, the first president of Angola – and the man who led the Popular Movement for the Liberation of Angola (MPLA) until his death in 1979. The leader of this unsuccessful coup, which took place in May of 1977, was Nito Alves, an MPLA dissident and a pro-Soviet who served as the Interior Minister of Angola from 1975 to 1976.[15]

The consequence of that failed coup was the persecution of Alves's sympathizers and the death of thousands of people. Supposedly, Comissão das Lágrimas was an organization created with the purpose of interrogating and torturing intellectual figures who had supported the rebellion. In *Comissão das Lágrimas*, Lobo Antunes gives account of several arrests and murders. Police cars transport anonymous suspects to São Paulo prison in Luanda. Wearing ragged uniforms and worn-out shoes – thus not being able to conceal their own miserable condition – police and military officers prone to cruelty ask the same questions repeatedly and torture detainees. The author also makes various references to crowds of prisoners, to seas of bruised, battered, and unrecognizable dead bodies (Atunes 2011, 32). Even though Lobo Antunes never runs the risk of compromising his work with historiographical interpretations, the reader assumes that Comissão das Lágrimas and the Angolan authorities are behind that chaos.

Accused of being members of Comissão das Lágrimas, figures such as Pepetela or Luandino Vieira deny the existence of any organization created to incarcerate and torture those who supported Alves's rebellion (Pepetela Jan 16, 2012). Since this is still a subject that needs further research and historiographical clarification, one will abstain from making considerations about this historical event. Nonetheless, one of the aims of this article is to provide some answers to the following questions: How does the writer describe this complex period of Angolan history? How can fiction help readers apprehend the complexities of history? What are the boundaries between reality and fiction in Lobo Antunes's work?

In an interview from 2010, Lobo Antunes declared that he was writing a book based on the final days of Elvira, or "Virinha", a leading member of the Angolan Army. As a matter of fact, it is of public knowledge that, due to her participation in the rebellion against Agostinho Neto's government, the authorities tortured and killed this woman (Coutinho 2010). Throughout *Comissão das Lágrimas*, the reader comes across a recurrent scene in which members of that referred commission torture a female who sings uninterruptedly. Although her name is never mentioned, Virinha is that woman who resists her perpetrators by singing. Once again, when writing about this organization, one can only speculate, and that applies to Virinha's resistance to torture. Even so, Lobo Antunes's worries don't have a clear connection with facts or factual history.

---

[15] Nito Alves, a hardcore Marxist-Leninist who supported Fractionism, opposed the rising influence of Maoism on MPLA's policies.

Knowing whether Virinha was singing while being tortured isn't that relevant for the writer, since his main determination is to apprehend the essence of past events. More essential for him is the characterization of life in Angola from his subjective points of view. That means that Virinha is not even a relevant character in this novel. She is a representation of the nonsensical violence, stupidity, and savagery that affected everyone who had the misfortune of living in Angola after the end of the war: politicians, soldiers, high-ranked military officers, and, of course, millions of ordinary people. Therefore, the main theme of this book is violence and destruction, and the alienation and insanity resulting from that devastation. To be more accurate, the central topic of this novel is not Comissão das Lágrimas but life itself, the meaning of life. In any case, one should underline the idea that Lobo Antunes digs into an Angolan historical theme to meditate upon human decadence in its many forms. Following the structure of previous novels, he writes about a family that was torn apart by war, crimes, betrayals, lies, and viciousness. That family is, however, a microcosm of Portugal, a country that came across a dreadful humiliation in Africa.

Comissão das Lágrimas is a fictional report of a limit-experience that occurred in Angola two years after the end of the Colonial War. The voice or character chosen by Lobo Antunes to report that limit-experience is Cristina, a woman in her mid-forties who writes her memories from a psychiatric hospital in Portugal. Living in a world where reality combines with fantasy, this mentally deranged person recreates her fragmented childhood in Angola, during the Colonial War, from the perspective of someone who is not able to understand the events and the people surrounding her. Cristina hears voices, interacts with objects and artifacts from another era, and schizophrenically dives into a past where her parents assume key importance. She inhabits a swampy reality that compels her to digress into diverse layers of the past.[16] Despite the vagueness of her discourse, it is through Cristina's lenses that one finds out that Alice, her mother, used to work in a brothel with the artistic name of Simone. It is also through Cristina that one learns that her father – maybe the most important character of this novel, since he's a member of Comissão das Lágrimas – is a timid, black ex-seminarist who never speaks. Tormented by homoerotic experiences or sexual abuses that occurred when he was studying to become a

---

[16] The narrator looks inside, revisits hidden places in her memory, and experiences intense emotions as if she could relive the past. Evelyn B. Fernandes observes that Lobo Antunes's characters usually lose themselves in a labyrinth of ghosts and feelings by immerging in their own memories. Evelyn Fernandes, "A ficção de António Lobo Antunes: da coreografia dos espectros à caligrafia dos afectos," PhD dissertation, (Universidade de Coimbra, 2015), 27.

priest, her father is driven by strong desires of revenge (Špánková 2014, 233). This character's silence may be a symbol for repressed emotions: silence is a consequence of barbarism. In the spirit of Adorno's famous quote – the philosopher pronounced that to write a poem after Auschwitz was barbaric [17]– Lobo Antunes demonstrates in this novel that words lose validity when mankind comes across the most devastating calamities.[18] Furthermore, this character's silence is a metaphor for the dubious existence of Comissão das Lágrimas. More than once, several unnamed characters – members of Comissão das Lágrimas – torture, interrogate, and intimidate detainees with accusations such as the following: "You were trying to sell out your country to the colonialists, to the South Africans, to the Chinese, and to the Russians."[19] Cristina's father stands out for his cruelty, and the long list of atrocities committed by him is insurmountable. An example of this is the passage where he has sexual intercourse with a dead body (Špánková 2014, 235).

Cristina is outside the real world. Suffering from a mental disease – maybe dementia or schizophrenia – she is the ideal person to narrate her family's shattered past. First, because she does not have the credibility to accurately report her father's actions. She hints that her black father was a member of Comissão das Lágrimas without making clear statements. She comes up with some fragments and visions of her father interrogating and beating prisoners, and sees torturers hanging a woman on a hook, smashing her face against the concrete floor, putting a bullet in her chest, and ripping out her nose. She also remembers witnessing this dying woman singing, just like Virinha (Atunes 2011, 235). Cristina recalls the explosions of bombs, the sound of rifles shooting, all kinds of destruction, but she isn't sure about anything, since the past is foggy. For that reason, she is the perfect character to describe a historical event that even today is at the center of intense discussions. By using a mentally ill character to tell the story of Comissão das Lágrimas, Lobo Antunes protects himself from possible historical misinterpretations or incorrections. Additionally, Cristina fits into Lobo Antunes's narrative techniques, especially into the dispersed way of recounting the past through a polyphonic symphony. In consonance with Daniel E. Colón's summarization of Lobo Antunes's narrative mode, one could argue that characters provide their individual and intimate viewpoints, which have numerous jumps in time and space, and do

---

[17] See T. Adorno, *Prisms* (Mass.: MIT Press, 1981).
[18] Writing about traumatic events will never give full account of what really happened in terms of suffering and destruction.
[19] The translation to English is mine. Antunes, *Comissão das Lágrimas*, 41.

not necessarily have a logical sequence.[20] On a slightly different note, one could also affirm that there isn't a plurality of narrators or characters in *Comissão das Lágrimas*, but an undetermined narrator who speaks in the first person and assumes a heterogeneity of intonations and colors. In any case, this ambiguity and nebulousness that makes it difficult to distinguish characters and to recount the past, prompted some critics to conclude that what prevails in this kind of narrative is the complexity and beauty of the text – in other words, the flow of writing (Gil 2004, 160).

In *Os Romances de Lobo Antunes*, Maria Alzira Seixo observes that the feeling of emptiness is omnipresent in Lobo Antunes's work, especially in his African novels, where emotional and physical degradation, as well as the abjection that derives from war, are constant (Sexio 2002, 54). Emptiness overshadows personalities, professions, families, and love affairs. This is particularly accurate in *Comissão das Lágrimas*, a book in which pain, anguish, and isolation undermine the possibilities of living normally. Cristina is a lost creature and confuses the past with the present. In her mind, Angola is a synonym for savagery, brutality, and massacres. Her descriptions of her parents are vague and imprecise. Even names seem to be devoid of meaning: names become faces, faces become gestures, gestures give way to ghosts, and the world turns into emptiness.

Every step these characters take is followed by desolation. First, places that used to be crowded and productive – factories, bars, offices, buildings – are now empty. Even natural elements, such as trees and flowers, lack vital energy and reveal darkness. For example, the Sun "silently" illuminates a mango tree. Misery is latent, characters lead depressing existences, even their appearance denotes decay and precarity. Alice, Cristina's mother, who is also Simone (a prostitute), suffers due to loneliness, to her husband's disaffection, and thinks that life in Angola is terrible because the country is hostile and suffocates white Portuguese people. Cristina also states that living in Angola is disturbing. Angola is a taciturn place where no one communicates freely: there is the sickening silence of her parents, the silence of Angolans, the silence of objects. People live in a perpetual state of confusion. Chaos is a debilitating force and emptiness is ubiquitous (Atunes 2011, 121). Impersonating solitude, Cristina and her mother–who sometimes seem to assume the same voice in the

---

[20] Colón also states that another way in which Lobo Antunes's portrays the "complex processes of human thought" is by constantly repeating key phrases and events: the effect of repetition emphasizes the magnitude and importance of certain traumatic events. Daniel Colón, "Analysis of the Narrative Structure and Style of *O Manual dos Inquisidores*: an allegory of the Salazar dictatorship in Portugal," *Hispanófila, Ensayos de Literatura*, nº 163 (2017): 66.

narrative–look back and see vultures, repressed feelings, and shadows. Cristina and her mother deal with depression. Angola is a desolate and meaningless country that prevents people from evolving and finding contentment. The background of this novel is undoubtedly Comissão das Lágrimas, the violence perpetrated by the members of this organization. Nonetheless, after reflecting upon the behaviors of these torturers, one concludes that what drives their actions is also suffering. For example, one "commissary" confesses that they–torturers, Angolans, everyone–no longer exist, that things ceased to make sense, that people are dying in vain because they are already dead: they are torturing "specters."[21]

Lobo Antunes gives special prominence to Angola's decrepit reality by pointing out physical elements of his characters that unveil signs of ugliness, indigence, and putrefaction. By way of illustration, he alludes to Alice's "dark roots of blonde dyed hair."[22] Alice's slovenly appearance is an example of how people lose touch with the real world in times of intense distress. Vanity becomes irrelevant and gives way to apathy. Why does Alice suffer? For many reasons: because her life is miserable, because Angola is not a Portuguese colony anymore, because a huge black void consumes her to the point that the word beauty stops making sense. Finally, because she is not black – she is a white Portuguese, unlike her "black husband", and her mind doesn't live in Angola but in Lisbon.[23] Comissão das Lágrimas, the organization, is a big mystery in this novel. Despite the recurrent references to police officers, torturers, and killers, there is always one question that the different characters repeat throughout the book: "Is your husband a member of Comissão das Lágrimas?" Officers constantly question Alice/Simone, but she shrugs her shoulders, and states that she doesn't even know what Comissão das Lágrimas is. Everything is strange to this woman: Angola, Angolans, her husband – whose name she never mentions – her daughter, Comissão das Lágrimas.[24] Cristina and her mother are always questioning the meaning of things. Pain and trauma explain their mental confusion. As a matter of fact, that pain only allows them to partially apprehend the meanings provided by reality: external events are too complex and painful to be converted into logical, structured narratives. Characters can only share their own fragmented dreams of the past.

As mentioned before, racism and all kinds of prejudice pervade Lobo Antunes's fiction. However, it is obvious that racism is less a reflection of the writer's beliefs than a portrayal of the mentality of the Portuguese who lived in

---

[21] Ibid., 155.
[22] Ibid., 21.
[23] Ibid., 23.
[24] Ibid., 25.

Angola and thought of themselves as a superior race. Aside from putting in evidence the arrogance of the colonizers, the characters' racism underlines the evidence that Portugal and its ex-colony are worlds apart. Cristina repeats that Angola is a distant place, and her mother frequently states that she is a white woman, that she should not have to deal with the problems of Angolans, that after the country's independence, no Portuguese should be in Angola being treated as if they were equal to those miserable people.[25] Alice rejects blacks for their blackness, for being different. Due to unexplained reasons, she is married to that mysterious member of Comissão das Lágrimas. Much of her bitterness comes from that dysfunctional relationship with her husband, and when she describes him, she confesses her own surprise at being attached to a black man whose stinky odor permeates her clothes and everything else, including her soul.[26] Alice also exclaims that she is "tired of blacks",[27] that blacks disgust her, that she doesn't even know why her black husband wastes his time chasing other miserable blacks.[28]

Another noteworthy character is mister Figueiredo, a white Portuguese businessman who owns the brothel that employed Cristina's mother before Angola's independence. Throughout the novel, Cristina, as well as other undistinguishable voices included in the narrative, imply that Figueiredo is Cristina's real father, not the unnamed black member of the so-called Comissão das Lágrimas. No less racist than his compatriots, this Portuguese businessman denies being Cristina's father, since her ugliness proves that she is the daughter of the "Black man."[29] When the Angolan authorities go after him and close his businesses, mister Figueiredo desperately begs Alice's husband – member of Comissão das Lágrimas – to help him, but the latter tells him that he cannot be of any help, that Figueiredo should forget his businesses and go back to Penafiel, in Portugal. [30] Forced to ask a favor to an Angolan, Figueiredo questions himself: "I never imagined asking favors to a Black."[31]

Thus, although the racism of these characters is notorious – as in other Lobo Antunes novels – it seems obvious that they are less concerned with their racial uniqueness, or superiority, than with the evidence that they belong to a country that used to be internationally respected. The problem here is one of identity: being Portuguese, longing to be in Lisbon, these characters feel repulsion for a

[25] Ibid., 39.
[26] Ibid., 145.
[27] Ibid., 82.
[28] Ibid., 77.
[29] Ibid., 75.
[30] Ibid., 73.
[31] Ibid., 71.

place that has only shown them disgrace, poverty, and destruction. This novel is all about annihilation, mental, cultural, and social destruction. Having to live with that heavy burden, having experienced war, disappointment, having seen many people die, these characters feel deprived of their identity: they have forgotten who they are. Cristina's father, the unnamed man known for his blackness – even his wife calls him black – is the perfect example of this loss of identity. He is a virulent creature nurtured by revengeful instincts, and tortures and chases innocent people. However, there comes an ulterior moment in the narrative when the authorities chase him for being a member of Comissão das Lágrimas, and he becomes a prisoner instead of a torturer. Torturers ask him if he wants to bring the Portuguese back in Angola, or if he is a traitor with desires of seeing colonialism reinstated.[32] This man is a representation of trauma: he was sexually abused, he tortures and kills people, he has sexual intercourse with a dead body. After all, he is no one. He is nothing, he has no identity.

Lobo Antunes moves back and forth, digresses between different chronological periods, but the most important point to retain is that no one experiences real happiness in this story. Lobo Antunes presents Comissão das Lágrimas as an organization driven by nihilistic motivations: the novel ends as it starts, with devastation, with voices complaining about life in Angola, or about irrelevant fights and wars that lead nowhere.

As was said before, Cristina hears voices, and dispersion and fragmentation characterize her narrative. She oscillates between multiple layers of the past and the present. Consequently, it is difficult to make sense of her recollections. In most occasions, Cristina barely describes her visions. For instance, she remembers seeing dead bodies, naked black people tied up with wire and being tortured.[33] She only provides the reader with dispersed images. Constantly reproduced both by Cristina and her mother, these visions of Angolans being tortured symbolize the impossibility of inhabiting a place devastated by the horrors of war. Memory works here as a blocking energy that prevents people from existing in the present. This incapacity to be in the present drives this novel's characters to destructive behaviors: adultery, rape, prostitution, mental illnesses, and substance abuse. Despite narrating her own past, it is challenging to contextualize and give coherence to Cristina's words. Since the reader never knows what really happened or what is going to happen next – the narrative only offers some glimpses of reality – one must infer from what is told that the novel deals with a specific and traumatic historical event: Comissão das Lágrimas and the killing of thousands of people. This novel also deals with recurring topics in Lobo Antunes's oeuvre. One of those topics is family and

---

[32] Ibid., 63.
[33] Ibid., 19.

incommunicability – or the disintegration of family, and its connection to diffused memories of shattered and chaotic relationships. Other themes are mental disease[34] and the objectification and dehumanization of women.[35]

Comissão das Lágrimas is not a realistic novel and the intention of its author was not to produce historical fiction. So one can only conclude that this book does not offer a contribution to understanding whether this organization or commission existed. In that sense, one could easily accept that Lobo Antunes's referred work doesn't interpret reality – at least, factual reality. Nevertheless, Lobo Antunes interprets reality from a psychological perspective–he is interested in exploring, for example, the trauma caused by war. The writer analyzes decadence from the inside, from the depths of the Portuguese soul. As in other African novels, in *Comissão das Lágrimas* it is possible to find a multitude of beings who lost their identity. This is how he describes Portuguese and Africans: no one exists after so much destruction and sadness.

Works cited

Adorno, Theodor W. *Prisms*. Mass.: MIT Press, 1981.

Antunes, António Lobo. *Comissão das Lágrimas*. Lisbon: D. Quixote, 2011.

___. "Não tenho muito jeito para viver." *Visão*. November 20, 2014. http://visao.sapo.pt/actualidade/cultura/antonio-lobo-antunes-nao-tenho-muito-jeito-para-viver=f802105.

Arnaut, Ana Paula. "A escrita insatisfeita e inquieta (nte) de António Lobo Antunes." In *A Arte do Romance*, ed. by Felipe Cammaert, 71-88. Lisbon: D. Quixote, 2011.

Bakhtin, M. *Questões de literatura e de estética*. São Paulo: EDUNESC, 1990.

Blanco, María Luisa. *Conversaciones con António Lobo Antunes*. Madrid: Ediciones Siruela, 2001.

Cammaert, Felipe. "You don't invent anything: memory and the patterns of fiction in Lobo Antunes's work." In *Facts and Fictions of António Lobo Antunes*, ed. by Victor K. Mendes, 267-289. Massachusetts: UMass Dartmouth, 2017.

Cardina, Miguel. "Luta ca caba inda: from archive to fragment."

Colón, Daniel. "Analysis of the Narrative Structure and Style of *O Manual dos Inquisidores:* an allegory of the Salazar dictatorship in Portugal." *Hispanófila, Ensayos de Literatura* 163 (2017): 63-78.

---

[34] *Comissão das Lágrimas* is not the first book in which Lobo Antunes gives account of people with mental problems. For example, in *Arquipélago da Insónia* (2008) the protagonist is an autist man who revisits his childhood from a hospice room.

[35] In the writer's fiction, women are animalesque, and they suffer at the hands of men: they are raped and tortured. Evelyn Fernandes, 40.

Conrad, Peter. "Doctor and Patient. A Portuguese novelist dissects his country." *New Yorker,* May 4, 2009: 69-73. https://www.newyorker.com/magazine/2009/05/04/doctor-and-patient.

Coutinho, Isabel. "Virinha e Comissão das Lágrimas andam na cabeça de Lobo Antunes." *Público,* May 1, 2010. www.publico.pt/2010/05/01/jornal/virinha-e-comissao-das-lagrimas-andam-na-cabeca-de-lobo-antunes-19308994.

David, Isabel. "The retornados: trauma and displacement in post-revolution Portugal." *Etniskumo Studijos* 2 (2015): 114-130.

Fernandes, Evelyn Blaut. "A ficção de António Lobo Antunes: da coreografia dos espectros à caligrafia dos afectos." PhD dissertation, Universidade de Coimbra, 2015.

Fernández, Daniel de. "Os *retornados* with Antunes: Luanda, Angola and Lisbon." *Irish Journal for Culture, Arts, Literature and Language* 1, article 19 (2016). http://arrow.dit.ie/priamls/vol1/iss1/19.

Gil, José. *Portugal, Hoje: o Medo de Existir.* Lisboa: Relógio d´Água, 2004.

___. "Fechamento e linhas de fuga em Lobo Antunes." In *A Arte do Romance,* ed. by Felipe Cammaert, 157-170. Lisbon: D. Quixote, 2011.

Gomes, Álvaro et al. "A História como paródia: a revisitação da era das conquistas por António Lobo Antunes." *Revista Let* 1 (2017): 13-25.

Gould, Isabel A. Ferreira. "Ficções do eu colonial e pós-imperial: memória, identidade e família em *O Esplendor de Portugal.*" In *Facts and Fictions of António Lobo Antunes,* ed. by Victor K. Mendes, 151-178. Massachusetts: UMass Dartmouth, 2017.

Guerreiro, António. "Quem falou em polifonia?" *Expresso, Actual,* nº 2033, October, 2011.

Humphrey, Robert. *Stream of Consciousness in the Modern Novel.* London: University of California Press, 1972.

Madureira, Luís. "The discreet seductiveness of the Crumbling Empire: sex, violence, and colonialism in the fiction of António Lobo Antunes." *Luso-Brazilian Review* 32. 1 (1995): 17-30.

Moutinho, Isabel. "Writing the War and the Man in the first Novels of António Lobo Antunes." In *Facts and Fictions of António Lobo Antunes,* ed. by Victor K. Mendes, 71-87. Massachusetts: UMass Dartmouth, 2017.

Oliveira, Silvana Maria Pessoa. "Relendo as naus portuguesas–ironia e paródia na obra de Lobo Antunes." *SCRIPTA* 4, nº 8 (2001): 295-302.

Pepetela. "27 de Maio de 1977 e Nito Alves–o Tabu da História de Angola." Interview by João Carlos. *DW,* May 14, 2012. www.dw.com/pt-002/n%C3%A3o-houve-nenhuma-comiss%C3%A3o-das-l%C3%A1grimas-em-angola-diz-pepetela/a-15949744.

___. "Não se festeja a morte de ninguém." Interview by Rita Freire. *Buala. Cultura contemporânea Africana,* Jan. 16, 2012. www.buala.org/pt/cara-a-cara/nao-se-festeja-a-morte-de-ninguem-entrevista-a-pepetela.

Seixo, Maria Alzira. *Os Romances de António Lobo Antunes, Análise, interpretação, resumos e guiões de leitura.* Lisbon: D. Quixote, 2002.

___. "Still Facts and Living Fictions." In *Facts and Fictions of António Lobo Antunes,* ed. by Victor K. Mendes, 19-44. Massachusetts: UMass Dartmouth, 2017.

Špánková, Silvie. "O tema do trauma em *Comissão das Lágrimas* de António Lobo Antunes e *Estação das Chuvas* de José Eduardo Agualusa." *Études romanes de Brno* 35 (2014): 225-236.

Vargas Llosa, Mario. *Cartas a un joven novelista*. Madrid: Alfaguara, 2011.

Williams, Raymond Leslie. *Mario Vargas Llosa: a life of writing*. Texas: Univ. of Texas, 2014.

Zenith, Richard. "The geographer's manual: the place of place in António Lobo Antunes." In *Facts and Fictions of António Lobo Antunes*, ed. by Victor K. Mendes, 133-142. Massachusetts: UMass Dartmouth, 2017.

Chapter 3

Women Writing Men: Representations of Men and Masculinity in the Works of Lília Momplé, Paulina Chiziane and Ana Paula Tavares

Margret Chipara and Martha Mzite
University of Zimbabwe

Abstract

This chapter seeks to contribute to discourse on literature in Lusophone Africa by carrying out a comparative analysis of representations of men and masculinity in the literary works of Lília Momplé and Paulina Chiziane of Mozambique and Ana Paul Tavares of Angola. Lusophone Africa has been accorded relatively little scholarly attention on the African continent, where literary scholarship tends to be separated by geo-linguistic boundaries and dominated by Francophone and Anglophone scholars. Drawing from postcolonial, feminist and hegemonic masculinity theories, the chapter will examine the female perspective of male figures and masculinity, touching on, among other things, the patriarchal male figure; representations of the male body and male sexuality; representations of male behavior and male relationships with others. The chapter will also interrogate how these female writers engage with and question issues of manliness, male deviance and male hegemony.

Keywords: masculinity, patriarchy, gender, male sexuality, manliness

* * *

Introduction

For centuries, issues relating to the status of women and girls have stimulated fierce debate the world over. In Africa, although women form the majority of the population, their social, economic and political status remains largely and relatively inferior to that of men. It is against this backdrop that this chapter analyses masculinity and maleness in Lusophone literature. This literature has tended to be predominantly male-authored and to present primarily strong male protagonists in opposition to stereotypically submissive, passive female characters who accept their destiny in a largely patriarchal society. This chapter analyzes the extent to which the so-called crisis of masculinity has impacted on and is reflected in Lusophone African literary texts. Specific reference will be made, in this regard, to Momplé's Ninguém matou Suhura (1998), selected poems by Paula Tavares and Paulina Chiziane's Niketche: uma historia da poligamia (2002). The aforementioned texts were selected because their authors in whose works feature a range of minor and major male characters. Moreover, their storylines represent Lusophone African society during the colonial (in the case of Momplé) and postcolonial contexts. These authors therefore present a microcosm of various scenarios in which masculinity can be observed as male characters interacting amongst themselves and with female characters, even as the writers and readers interact with the text.

Literature Review

Masculinity studies have received increasing scholarly attention in recent years. Groes-Green notes that such studies include Kurtz (1996), Connell and Messerschimidt (2005), Goody (1976), Arnfred (2004), Amadiume (1987), and Arndt et al (2006). Connell (2005) advocates for a re-thinking of masculinities that includes theoretical perspectives from the global South. This scholar avers that masculinities do not necessarily relate to men but rather to their position within the gender order. There are multiple, internally complex, contradictory and constantly changing masculinities, and women play a role in their formation as they interact with men and boys.

Morrell and Swart (2005) examine the multiple ways in which masculinities are constructed as well as the position and behavior of men in the postcolonial world. They consider how colonialism impacted on men and manliness, transforming the societal roles of men. Following McClintock (1995), they opine that fully understanding colonialism and postcolonialism requires an appreciation of the relationship between race, gender and class; to examine the masculinity of black men requires an appreciation of the relationship between masculinity, sexuality and power (Morrell and Swart 2005, 96) and that "[t]he power of men over women is a foundation of their masculinity" (Morrell and Swart 2005, 107).

For Aboim (2009, 201), meanwhile, male and masculine identities should be examined from the perspective of globalization processes, acknowledging how masculinities are constantly reshaped "both by macro-level institutional, political and economic changes and through micro-level agency and reinterpretation." Such changes are impacting many traditionally patrilineal African societies and the roles of men and women therein.

The issue of power emerges in Groes-Green's (2009) study of hegemonic and subordinated masculinities amongst Mozambican men. This scholar finds that while middle class men use financial power, those who are unemployed and lack the financial means "enact masculinities that are subordinate vis-à-vis middle class peers, but which find expression through violence or sexual performance vis-à-vis female partners" (Groes-Green 2009, 286), as means of asserting their manhood and power (Groes-Green 2009, 98). The sexualization of masculinity is based on the male's ability to sexually satisfy women and violent tendencies against women are transmitted intergenerationally and intended to put women in their traditionally prescribed place (Groes-Green 2009, 294).

Fonchingong (2006, 134-135) considers the gender dimension in pre-colonial, colonial and postcolonial African literature, examining how men and women have been depicted therein and how female characters are now being depicted in contemporary literature. Lugarinho (2017, 143), meanwhile, examines masculinities in the literatures of Lusophone African countries. This scholar notes how masculine identity is being constantly transformed culturally, historically, geographically and socially and how societal structures have been disrupted by the advent of modernity and capitalism (Lugarinho 2017, 141-142), resulting in a re-definition of gender order (2017, 150). The identities of colonized African males, for instance, were transformed in their relations with the colonizer (Lugarinho 2017, 142-143). Indeed, with colonialism, they occupied a subaltern position as accomplices or were marginalized, while the white European male tended to be viewed as the paradigm of masculinity, superior and imbued with humanity, while the subjugated peoples were viewed as lacking humanity and authentic masculinity, and therefore effeminate or child-like (Lugarinho 2013, 19). Lugarinho (2013, 16) also makes the very apt observation that the traditional emphasis on the literary representations of female identities has resulted in the homogenization of masculine identities, disregarding the historical and cultural circumstances that have made them multiple and plural.

Sabine (2010, 187), meanwhile, specifically examines the emasculation and the crisis of the Negro patriarch in *Nós Matámos o Cão Tinhoso* by Mozambican writer Luís Bernardo Honwana. Following Connell's (2005) masculinities theory, he argues that the Lusotropicalist ideology of racial democracy peddled by the Portuguese colonial regime necessitated both "oppressive hierarchies of race and gender, and the need to efface the indigenous patriarch so as to sustain the myth of Portuguese 'civilization' and propagation in a 'savage' Africa." Colonial authority was therefore associated with hegemonic colonial masculinity and marginalizing indigenous masculinity. Black men were labelled as inadequate or aberrant, hiding the brutality of colonial patriarchy, which practised an unchecked physical and sexual violence against both subordinated male groups (Sabine 2010, 189). Sabine argues that Honwana ironically attributes to civil(izing) white colonial males the characteristics that they attribute to the colonized black males: sexual depravation and violent rage. Subordination excluded indigenous males from exercising hegemonic masculinity, objectifying them as bestial, infantile or effeminate (Sabine, 2010, 193). Complicity by colonized males (and females) was also necessary to ensure one's status within Mozambican colonial society, which was controlled by those at the top of the social hierarchy.

Theoretical Framework

The theoretical underpinnings of this chapter are drawn primarily from Connell's Masculinities. This scholar defines the world gender order as "the structure of relationships that interconnect the gender regimes of institutions, and the gender orders of local societies, on a world scale" (2005, xxi). The gender orders of different societies have been brought into contact by imperialism and neo-colonialism, which could explain the connection between the construction of masculinity and the construction of racial and ethnic hierarchies (2005, xxii). Connell also sees an intricate link between masculinity, institutional history, economic structures and social organization.

Connell defines masculinity as "a place in gender relations, the practices through which men and women engage that place in gender, and the effect of these practices on bodily experience, personality and culture" (2005, 71), observing how institutions such as the state, the workplace and the home are substantively gendered. Moreover, there are multiple masculinities "within a single nation" not to mention globally (…), and the "relations of alliance, dominance and subordination" between these multiple masculinities are built on "practices that exclude and include, that intimidate and exploit (…)". Moreover, the gender relations within "the milieu of class and race need to be unpacked and scrutinized" (2005, p. 76). Another important point that Connell makes is that a particular hegemonic masculinity is not fixed, but may be contested or reversed, giving rise to another or others.

Momplé's *Ninguém Matou Suhura*

The first story of this collection, 'Aconteceu em Saua-Saua', is set in the Mozambican colonial period. It recounts the story of Mussa Racua, the male protagonist, who is desperate to borrow some rice in order to fulfill the quota of rice required to be submitted to the colonial administration. The penalty for failing to do so is forced labor in the dreaded plantation, which Mussa Rucua believes will be the fate of many men in this particular year. Having experienced life in the plantation before, he is certain of one thing: that he could not survive the experience again. "Não sei nada! Só sei que não aguento a plantação segunda vez" (Momplé 1988, p.11). Momplé allows her readers into the mind of her male protagonist to understand the social, economic and psychological realities of the colonized Mozambican or Lusophone African male that he represents.

Mussa Racua symbolizes the powerlessness of the colonized Mozambican male, deprived of his malehood and humanity. He is powerless to determine his own destiny and has virtually no control of his life, having been forced once already and at risk of being forced again to work in the plantations. The first time he had been forced to work in the sisal plantation of Senhor Fonseca, he had been exposed to inhuman conditions characterized by insufficient time to sleep in mosquito-infested, shared sleeping quarters and whippings (Momplé 1988, 15). The whip or chicote was an instrument of repression, through which the colonizing male exerted and maintained his power. One also sees the psycho-social effect of forced plantation life on the families and marriages of the colonized male. Not only are families deprived of a breadwinner and provider of material and other means, but a young male may even lose his wife, as Mussa Racua did his first wife.

Owing, perhaps, to Mussa Racua's socialization as an African male making him internalize his feelings, he is unable or unwilling to externalize his feelings and the traumatic experiences associated with plantation life. He opts to take his own life rather than confiding in his pregnant second wife and returning to the plantation to be treated like an animal only to return home and find that his wife has left him for another man. Once again, the reader is allowed to access his thoughts:

> Não, não posso aguentar outra vez tanto sofrimento ----pensa ele----há outros que aguentam, mas eu não posso. É melhor morrer. Não acordar nunca mais. Não ser mais um animal. Não ver mais um animal. Não voltar mais a casa a ver que a minha mulher já foi com outro homem. (Momplé 1988, 16)

The other 'male' in the story 'Aconteceu em Saua-Saua' takes the form of the colonial administrative structures, "a Administração." It represents an entire system – made up primarily of white colonizing males – closely linked to the plantation. Together, the administration and the plantation represent the political and economic power which weighs down on the lives of colonized Mozambican males such as Mussa Racua. Administrative officials, all of whom are male in Momple's Ninguém matou Suhura, remain nameless and are presented as heartless and indifferent to the circumstances of colonized people. This is evident in their demand to receive the stipulated quota of rice from the colonized males – which they determine arbitrarily – even when the latter are unable to do so owing to sickness, poor quality seed or poor rains. In fact, they benefit financially from the failure of the colonized males to submit the required quota of rice to send them to the plantations, assured of a payment from the plantation owners for each man – or free laborer – that they send to work on the plantations. Mussa Racua is well aware of this web of complicity: "os donos das plantações ficam contentes porque conseguem uma data de homens para trabalhar de graça. E a gente da Administração fica contente porque recebe dos donos das plantações um tanto por cabeça que entrega." (Momplé 1988, 12).

The Administration and those associated with it inspire tremendous fear in the colonized Mozambican male, as evidenced in the inability of the tattered man who later comes to report the suicide of Mussa Racua to control his trembling in the presence of the Administrator (Momplé 1988, 17). The Administrator's translator, a subordinated and likely assimilated male, enables communication between the uneducated colonized people and the colonial administrative system, effectively propping it up.

The callous indifference of the Administration is evident once again in the impatient manner in which the Administrator responds to the report of Mussa Racua's suicide. He is uninterested or rather irritated by what are, in his view, negro dramas (Momplé 1988,18). Indeed, he is more interested in the whereabouts of the rice that Mussa Racua was supposed to hand in than in his death, thereby further dehumanizing him, even in death. Contemptuously, he refers to Mussa Racua and those like him to dogs, a cursed race, who either flee from work or commit suicide (Momplé 1988, 18).

Another of Momplé's short stories, 'Caniço', narrated in the third person, also allows us into the thoughts and feelings of Naftal, and through him, the perspective of a young colonized Mozambican male. When the story begins, Naftal has been orphaned and forced to take over headship of his family at the age of 18 with the death of his migrant worker father. As the breadwinner, his father had often been away from his family, and his absence is sorely felt by Naftal and the entire family. During his rare visits, the family experiences relative abundance, suggesting that in his absence there is a lack. However, the time with his father is so brief and spaced out that in the period after, Naftal is always left feeling the bitterness of misery more intensely (Momplé 1988, 21).

The effect of tuberculosis that Naftal's father contracted in the South African mines symbolically renders him the antithesis of the strong African father figure. The illness and death of Naftal's father highlight the plight of colonized African males and their families. Naftal's father dies with little to show for all the effort and sacrifice he has made: a bundle of used clothes, a small radio and a pair of spectacles. "As minas tinham-lhe comido as forças e a carne, como a tantos outros negros que partem de Moçambique perseguindo sonhos de riqueza. E, depois de tantos anos de trabalho esgotante deixavam como herança uma trouxa de roupa usada, um pequeno rádio e um par de óculos" (Momplé 1988, 23). Using pathos, Momplé highlights the exploitation of the hapless colonized African male migrant laborers and the complicity of the Portuguese colonial regime and South African apartheid regime in this regard.

Through the eyes and mind of the young male narrator as he walks from his home in the shanty town to the plush white neighborhood in which he works, one also gains insight into the life that he leads as a colonized person. One senses the fear, dehumanization, segregation and resignation to his fate and that of others like him. They can only gaze longingly at things that they cannot have; in tattered clothes and without shoes, prohibited from sitting in the tea salons where they wait on tables. For this reason, he concludes that the negro is the brother of the dog – "Negro é mesmo irmão de cão!" (Momplé 1988, 27) – thereby animalizing himself and others like him.

Naftal's white male employer, o patrão, symbolic of the colonial regime, is presented in a negative light by Momplé. He represents the system's injustice when he wrongfully accuses Naftal and his elderly fellow worker, o cozinheiro, on mere suspicion of stealing his wife's watch and then has them punished. It is the patrão who has the power to decide their fate, handing them over to the police based on his conviction that one or both of them is/are guilty. The white police agent at the police station is complicit with and bolsters the unjust and oppressive system that the patrão represents. The description of his dirty gums – which are in evidence as he assures the patrão that the suspects will be 'squeezed' well – suggests that the writer has a negative attitude towards this character.

While the patrão enjoys his dinner in the comfort of his home, at the police station, Naftal and the elderly male cook are being subjected to arbitrary violence and dehumanized as the sipaio Abdulrazaque attempts to force confessions out of them. One witnesses the total humiliation of the elderly cozinheiro: he writhes and shouts in pain, as he is beaten on the palm like a naughty child (Momplé 1988, 30), and denied the respect and dignity generally accorded to him in African culture owing to his age. Having been physically abused, Naftal and the cozinheiro are verbally abused and referred to as large monkeys, "grandes macacos." Despite their injuries, they are warned to report to work the following day, as the patrão may need them. He has the power to have them detained again, if he so desires, highlighting the unchecked power that he has within this system and over the lives of these colonized males. In contrast to young males in some of the poems of Agostinho Neto or the short story "Dina" by Luis Bernardo Honwana, for example, Naftal is so beaten down that he has resigned himself to his condition as a colonized male, and makes no attempt to resist or fight against the system.

'Ninguém matou Suhura', despite its title, is focused not on the female character Suhura but on a white male protagonist, o *Sr Administrador*, who is the colonial administration personified. Once again, the reader is allowed to travel through the mind of this protagonist. Momplé's attitude towards this character is clear from the very start. Despite the clearly unflattering physical description of him provided by the writer, for example, o *Sr Administrador* is quite pleased with his physical appearance as he admires himself in the mirror. The discrepancy between, and juxtaposition of, his view and that of the writer is a source of humour.

> "A imagem que o espelho lhe devolve não lhe desagrada. A parte uma gordura incipiente na zona da cintura, o corpo conserva uma elegância maciça perfeitamente adequada aos seus quarenta e oito anos. O rosto também lhe parece aceitável; nem sequer repara nas bolsas flácidas e redor dos olhos e no duplo queixo que há anos se vem desenvolvendo e o fazem parecer-se vagamente com uma rã." (Momplé 1988, 49)

The humorously unflattering description of the *Sr Administrador* is extended further as his weight and size are unfavourably compared to those of the *puxador* who pulls his rickshaw. It is both literally and metaphorically significant that the *puxador*, another colonized Mozambican male, is animalized in the sense that, as a horse usually does, he draws the rickshaw in the scorching heat while the *Sr Administrador* does his errands. A clear contrast is drawn between the heaviness of *Sr Administrador* and the thinness of the *puxador*, whose limbs are deformed under the latter's over eighty kilos of weight (Momplé 1988, 52). Symbolically, the *puxador* may be viewed as representing the colonized Mozambican – and indeed African – beast of burden, crushed under the weight of colonialism.

The unfavorable portrayal of the *Sr Administrador* continues further as his mannerisms and tendencies are satirized. His ritualistic trajectory between his home to his palace – which he chooses to undertake by rickshaw rather than motorcar – enables him to enjoy both the sense of deference and terror he evokes in people. Likened to a king, he is described as distributing smiles, greetings and brief gestures, according to the category and race of those who greet him (Momplé, 1988, p. 53). This white colonial male, who clearly enjoys the attention and deference that his position of power affords him, is socially and racially discriminatory.

More sinister is the *Sr Administrador*'s abuse of his power to pick and choose women with whom he wishes to engage in adulterous sexual relations. His power extends beyond the life of the colonized male to that of the colonized female as well. His much-feared *sipaio Abdulrazaque*, a complicit colonized male, intimidates Suhura's grandmother into giving up her young virgin granddaughter to satisfy the *Sr Administrador*'s sexual desires. Momplé highlights his sense of entitlement to these women and their bodies in his threats of violence when he hears of the grandmother's initial refusal to give up her grandchild. "- Essa velha merecia umas boas palmatoadas. Onde se viu negar uma marusse ao administrador? Esta gente anda com a grimpa muito levantada"(Momplé 1988, 53).

The power that the *Sr Administrador* wields makes him a key part of the syndicated sexual exploitation of colonized women. Through his encounter with Suhura, one sees the dehumanization and objectification of any such woman who happens to take his fancy. This young girl, whose name he does not even know, is, in his view, nothing more than a beautiful black girl who passes through his hands, even less important than his pets. "O sr administrador nada sabe sobre a rapariga nem sequer o nome. É apenas mais uma bela negrinha que lhe passa pelas mãos, sem dúvida muito menos importante para ele que qualquers dos seus animais de estimação. Mas mesmo assim, é-lhe extremamente agradável saber que à tarde e terá à sua disposição, no discreto quartinho da D. Júlia Sá" (Momplé 1988, 54). Using dramatic irony, Momplé enables the reader to see beyond the outward appearance of the *Sr Administrador*: people who see him en route to D. Júlia Sá's house imagine that he is entertaining elevated thoughts, when these are, in actual fact, quite base and lustful (Momplé 1988, 60).

The *sipaio Abdulrazaque* and D. Júlia Sá, a black former prostitute, are therefore complicit in the syndicated sexual abuse and exploitation of Suhura. D. Júlia Sá emphasizes to Suhura's grandmother how fortunate she is that her granddaughter – a simple black girl of no value – has caught the fancy of a man as important as the *Sr Administrador* (Momplé 1988, 66-67). When D. Júlia Sá's entreaties fail to persuade Suhura's grandmother, Abdulrazaque threatens her for even daring to want to discuss the orders of the *Sr Administrador* (Momplé 1988, 67). The statements of these two characters reinforce the *Sr Administrador*'s power and great sense of entitlement.

The climax of the story is the rape and murder of Suhura, and it is here that the physical and political power of the *Sr Administrador* is most evident. Suhura, who had been initially resigned herself to her inevitable fate, changes her mind and decides that she cannot tolerate any physical contact with this stranger. There begins a physical battle as Suhura does all within her power to vehemently resist the attempts of the latter to force himself upon her. The combination of physical strength, overwhelming lust of the *Sr Administrador* and his rage that Suhura would dare to resist him is such that he rapes and kills her. However, this colonized female, likened to a caged animal, resists the colonizer to her death.

> Então a raiva que o sufoca atinge o auge. Já não sabe se quer possuir ou matar esta negrinha que ousa resistir à sua vontade e que, embora subjugada pelo seu corpo possante, estrebucha e morde como um animal encurralado. Por fim, usa toda a sua força, indiferente às consequências. (Momplé 1988, 70-71)

The Sr Administrador rapes and murders Suhura with impunity and without remorse, informing D. Julia that "O estupor da negra morreu!" Thereafter, he uses his henchman Abdulrazaque – who is accustomed to dealing with such 'unexpected" deaths – to dispose of Suhura's body and instill fear and impose silence, and offers protection to his other accomplice, D. Júlia (Momplé 1988, 70-71). The *sipaio* carries out his task efficiently; silencing Suhura's wailing grandmother with a threatening "Não grita, velha. Ninguém matou Suhura. Ninguém matou Suhura. Compreende?! (Momplé 1988, 72).

The power and sense of entitlement of the *Sr Administrador* are further in evidence in his relations with other subordinate males. By way of example, he commandeers free offers of new products from the fawning senior employee of Gulamo Nengy, one of the richest commercial houses in Ilha de Moçambique and later distributes these gifts to his wife and her friends (Momplé 1988, 55). Another subordinate white male who is part of the colonial administration is the *delegado da Mocidade Portuguesa*, a societal and institutional gatekeeper tasked to police the social behavior of the youth. It is for this reason that he does not approve of the fact that Manuela, the daughter of the *Sr Administrador*, treats colored students well, and even treats the black ones as if they were white (Momplé 1988, 59). He highlights the unacceptability of Manuela's closeness to the non-whites and threatens to take action against such behavior if it continues (Momplé 1988, 60).

The final story of Momplé's collection, 'O último pesadelo', is also dominated by a major white and minor black male characters. It begins with the white male protagonist, Eugénio, suffering in 1974 from nightmares triggered by the memories of traumatic events that he had witnessed in 1961, which took place at a hotel in colonial Angola inhabited by white colonists. The reader is taken back to those events through Momplé's use of the flashback technique, which enables the reader to understand and engage emotionally and empathetically with the story and the narrator's trauma.

Eugénio stands in stark contrast to most of the white male characters associated with the Portuguese colonial regime, who are portrayed negatively. Eugénio and the *agrimensor* he befriends are characterized positively as not being racially prejudiced, as are most of their white peers, in response to the rumors being circulated in the propagandist colonial media about the supposed misdeeds of the 'terrorists' (nationalists fighting for Angolan independence). The *agrimensor* chides his wife about her assumption that the insurgents are terrorists who cut off the ear, noses, etc. of all the whites they encounter (Momplé 1988, 77). Eugénio, too, remains objective and prefers not to air his views about these rumors, arousing the suspicions of other white males as to his loyalties (Momplé 1988, 78).

Indeed, in the short story 'O último pesadelo', the rumors spark fear and reinforce existing racial prejudices such that a group of twenty paranoid white males decide to gather up and neutralize the fourteen black employees of the hotel, for fear they will rise up against them, as the 'terrorists' are said to be doing in other parts of Angola. The whites encircle the blacks, who are likened to animals in a kraal, and beat them to death with large sticks. The brutality of this action is captured in the graphic description given by Momplé of the black employees trying to escape the strokes of the large sticks, blood gushing out of open wounds all over their bodies, especially their very swollen heads, hardly able to open their eyes and moving around blindly, trying to escape the beating. Meanwhile, the white males, who have formed a tight circle around them, are insulting them and egging on those who are beating them and one sadistic white male, Regalo, is standing at the entrance, holding a revolver, to ensure that none of the black employees escape (Momplé 1988, 78).

In contrast to the jeering white males, Eugénio is horrified and attempts in vain to dissuade his peers from taking justice into their own hands. However, threatened with the pistol and accused of being a traitor, he leaves the scene, helpless to assist the near-dead *velho Sabonete*, the black employee with whom he shared a sense of camaraderie. On the following day, he is challenged to prove his loyalty by shooting one of the blacks who is said to have escaped. This he refuses to do and abruptly leaves the hotel (Momplé 1988, 79-80).

When it is ultimately discovered that the alleged black conspiracy against the whites at the hotel was nothing more than a rumor, the white males involved in the murder of the black employees go unpunished, seemingly above the law. The deliberate use by Momplé, of the words "**todos os responsáveis** pelo **massacre**, mesmo os **assassinos**, tinham ficado impunes" (Momplé 1988, 82) amplifies the murderous nature of this event, highlighting the writer's attitude towards the perpetrators.

Paulina Chiziane's *Niketche: Uma historia de poligamia*

Niketche depicts the lives of Rami and her co-wives who fight for their rights in their polygamous family. The originally submissive wives are transformed into emancipated women against the will of Tony, their husband, the archetypal African male. In an at times humorous reversal of gender roles, they reduce him to a burdensome house husband as they become financially and sexually liberated.

The novel starts with an incident where Rami's son damages a stranger's car, but Tony is not available to resolve the issue with the car's owner. This suggests that Tony is an absentee husband and what Skinner et al. refer to as "non-resident" father (1999, 1). Luísa tells Rami, "Venho de uma terra onde os homens novos emigram e não voltam mais. A minha mãe nunca conseguiu um marido só para ela" (Chiziane 2002, 57), in reference to young Mozambican men's tendency to migrate and never return, resulting in a shortage and resultant sharing of men. It is this man shortage that enables Tony to appear in public to be in a monogamous marriage to Rami even as he maintains numerous extra-marital relationships with women drawn from various parts of Mozambique. Tony's status and appeal are associated with his apparent sexual prowess and position as chief of the police. His relationships produce children as numerous as "pumpkin seeds, multiplying by the dozen like a nest of mice" (Chiziane 2002, 97). His life revolves around gratifying his sexual desires and proving his manhood by the number of wives and children he has. When discussing different practices associated with marriage and sexuality with a love advisor, Rami declares: "o meu pai é um cristão ferrenho, de resto a pressão do regime colonial foi muito mais forte no sul do que no norte" (Chiziane 2002, 39). Being from the south, she is ignorant of what practices the other women do in order to safeguard their men. Rami is completely alien to initiation rites and polygamy due to her father's missionary work. She is therefore compelled to seek this information in order to keep her husband. Rami's conversation with the love counsellor shows how society teaches women how to keep a man by satisfying his love for food and sex: "prend[er]-o na cozinha e na cama" (Chiziane 2002, 45). Rami is advised to use the gizzard as a magic potion as this is what Mozambican men like the most (Chiziane 2002, 45). Ironically, Tony is not taught what to do to keep a woman and has been socialized to assume that it is women's responsibility to keep him satisfied.

Paradoxically, it is his desire for sex that proves to be Tony's undoing. As Mauá tells her co-wives, she is able to get Tony to do what she wants by threatening to go on sex strikes and forcing him on a sexual fast: "Ele fica atrapalhado e faz de tudo para me agradar" (Chiziane 2002, 181). His desire for sexual conquest is such that he fakes his own death in order to spend time in France with yet another girlfriend. This marks the beginning of Tony's demise. His death sparks off a chain of traditional rites that sees all his possessions, including his wives, being taken by his relatives. During this process, Tony's wives become active agents of their emancipation. They cease to be rivals to become a united front to challenge Tony and his family that uses patriarchy to oppress them and deny them a voice and space within their society.

Niketche progressively illustrates Tony's dwindling masculinity as the co-wives begin to assert themselves. Their financial independence – achieved through the *xitique* microcredit system –challenges his male authority as a breadwinner and provider. Tony's sexual role is taken over by his cousin through the *kutchinga* and challenged by Luisa, who has a male lover that she is willing to share with Rami, objectifying him. Indeed, Tony's power as an archetypal African male is taken from him as Rami and her co-wives make sexual demands of him, expecting him to satisfy them all at once.

The poetry of Ana Paula Tavares

In the poetry of postcolonial Angolan writer Ana Paula Tavares, the male is conspicuous in his absence and silence. Contrary to a literary tradition dominated by male writers and protagonists, Tavares' poems focus primarily on the female and the female body. The male presence is felt in what he does or does not do in relation to the female and the female body. In the poem "Não conheço nada do país do meu amado", for example, the female persona gives her beloved unfettered access to her life and her body, metaphorically referred to as *país*, as suggested by the lines "Abri-lhe as portas do meu país" and "Deixei que ele bebesse do meu país o vinho o mel a carícia." Although he enjoys the wine, honey and caress of her body, he appears to offer nothing in the form of information about himself or his origins or explanation about his whereabouts, as suggested by the lines "O meu amado não me disse nada do seu país" and "Nada me disse o meu amado." In fact, the words 'Volta com um cheiro de país diferente/Volta com os passos de quem não conhece a pressa' suggest that he comes and goes as he pleases and is promiscuous, since he often returns to the personae with the smell of another 'country' – taken here to be a metaphorical reference to another woman's body – and in no apparent hurry to be with her. As in some of Momplé's stories above, one detects a sense of entitlement, which is enabled by the female personae's openness and willingness to give him her all without question. She appears to desire intimacy, but he remains distant, evasive, unwilling to commit himself. Typically, in order for relationships to be successful, there needs to be give and take from both members. In the case here, she appears to be doing all of the giving while he is doing the taking.

The distant, non-responsive and non-committal behavior is evident in another poem, 'Amargos como os frutos'. Here, the beloved of the female persona returns a shadow of his former self, without footwear and with death in his eyes, as if inhabited by someone else. He no longer has the metal tongue on which her name was inscribed, and his voice is no longer as soft and sweet as it was before. Her beloved does not respond to any of the multiple questions that the persona asks, and his silence may leave the reader with many questions of his/her own.

In the poem 'Mirangolo', meanwhile, stereotypical notions associated with heterosexual male sexual performance are reinforced, with the male or the male organs being depicted as giving sexual pleasure and the female organs as avidly receiving it. The poem is simultaneously subtle and (porno)graphic in its description of the male sexual genitalia and sexual orgasm. Tavares plays on the literal meanings and possible sexual connotations evoked by certain words as she likens the adolescent male testicle to a mirangolo, a sweet purple fruit, whose acidic flavor of life cuts avid lips 'lábios ávidos', setting alight the wood and causing multiple 'feitiçarias do fogo', and changing into 'geleia real', a possible reference to the fluids resulting from sexual activity. Such references to the sexual organs and the sexual act tend to be taboo in many traditional patriarchal African societies, where Tamale (2006, 89) considers female sexuality in particular has been surveilled and repressed in a bid to maintain and enforce women's subordination. Although male sexuality and sexual performance may, in some contexts, be flaunted as markers of heterosexual maleness, in some traditional African societies, initiation rites associated with manhood are shrouded in secrecy and kept strictly between men. One imagines that a *female* poet writing about such an intimate part of the male body and the sexual act itself through such a public medium would be something of an unwelcome intrusion onto the male space.

In the poem 'História de amor da princesa Ozoro e do húngaro Ladislau Maygar', which is historico-biographical, patriarchal tendencies are very much in evidence. The King of Bié, the father of the female persona princess Ozoro, calls her to come and meet Ladislau Maygar, who is to be the lord of her life - 'senhor da tua vida/aquele que te fará árvore' – which suggests that the marriage has been arranged and Ozoro has had no choice in the matter. In effect, the lordship of the father is to be exchanged for that of the Hungarian explorer, who has asked for Ozoro's hand in marriage. The materialistic motives behind the father's decision are evident as he lists the items that have been paid by way of *lobolo* – cattle, fabric and hoes – by Ladislau, who has come from across the sea and is the colour of spirit. In fact, Ozoro's father has accepted the payment from this man without even knowing his clan of origin. Further on in the poem, Ladislau reveals that he is an explorer of gypsy origin. He brings to the kingdom of Bié horses and knowledge about wheat production in exchange for guides for new routes, food for caravans, authorization to go to Ochilombo and the hand in marriage of Ozoro, whom he hopes will cure him of fever and pain and teach him to be part of the land/kingdom.

In this poem, then, both Ozoro's father and Ladislau appear to be involved in a transaction in which Ozoro is one of the transacted commodities. In a sense, both Ozoro's father and Ladislau Maygar are complicit in a transaction involving Ozoro, from which both derive considerable benefit. That Ozoro's hand in marriage is last in Ladislau's list of priorities may be an indicator as to her position in that list. Indeed, the World Digital Library website suggests that Ladislau used his position as Ozoro's husband to gain access into the interior regions of Africa. In the poem, Ladislau anticipates the pleasure of his sexual encounter with the virigin Ozoro and the 'nest' that they will create together as he asks Ozoro 'Amada, deixa que prepare o melhor vinho .../e que, por casameno, me inicie/nas falas de uma terra que não conehço/no gosto de um corpo/que princípio.

Conclusion

This chapter examined how three Lusophone African women writers from Angola and Mozambique represent males and multiple forms of masculinity in their literary texts. These masculinities are evident in the interaction between male and female characters within the texts. Masculinities are hierarchical in nature and closely linked to physical, social and political power, and issues of race. They are sustained through the physical or psychological domination or abuse and exploitation of weaker or subordinate males and females. However, they may be resisted or challenged – with or without success – by the very same groups. Indeed, as seen in Chiziane's work, the resistance of subordinate female groups could result in a reversal of the traditional gender order. While Momplé challenges stereotypical representations of black and white males, Chiziane challenges stereotypical representations of females. Tavares, meanwhile, challenges stereotypically negative male behavior and potentially causes discomfort within the male socio-literary space with her presentation of the sexual male body.

Works Cited

Aboim, Sofia. "Men between Worlds: Changing Masculinities in Urban Maputo", *Men and Masculinities*, (2009) 12(2): 201-224.

Chiziane, Paulina. *Niketche: Uma historia de poligamia*. Lisboa: Editorial Caminho, 2002.

Connell, Raewyn. *Masculinities*. Berkeley and Los Angeles: University of California Press, 2005.

Fonchingong, Charles. "Unbending Gender Narratives in African Literature." *Journal of International Women's Studies*, 8(1): 135-147, 2006.

Groes-Green, Christian. "Hegemonic and Subordinated Masculinities: Class, Violence and Sexual Performance among Young Mozambican Men", *Nordic Journal of African Studies*, 18(4): 286-304. 2009.

Lugarinho, Mário. "Em direção ao 'Homem Novo' (Subsídios para os estudos de gênero e para os estudos pós-coloniais no contexto de Língua Portuguesa)", *Revista do Núcleo de Estudos de Literatura Portuguesa e Africana da UFF*, 5:10, 2013.

___. "Paradigmas confrontados: algumas masculinidades nas literaturas de língua portuguesa." *Metamorfoses*, 14: 141-151, 2017.

Momplé, Lília. *Ninguém Matou Suhura Maputo*. Associação dos Escritores Moçambicanos, 1988.

Moorman, Marissa. "Propaganda in Portugal's colonies: lessons for the West today." *The Conversation*, 2017. http://theconversation.com/propaganda-in-portugals-colonies-lessons-for-the-west-today-71106

Morrell, Robert, and Sandra Swart. "Men in the Third World: Postcolonial Perspectives on Masculinity." In Kimmel, M.S., Hearn, J. and Connell R.W. (eds) *Handbook of Studies on Men and Masculinities*, California, London, New Delhi: Sage Publications, 2005.

Sabine, Mark. "Nós Matámos o Cão-Tinhoso: A Emasculação de África e a Crise do Patriarca Negro." *Via Atlântica*, 1(17), 187-200, 2010.

Sutton, David. "Whole Foods: Revitalization through Everyday Synesthetic Experience." *Anthropology and Humanism* 25.2 (120–30), 2001.

Tamale, Sylvia. "Eroticism, Sensuality and 'Women's Secrets' among the Baganda", *IDS Bulletin*, 37.5, 2006, https://core.ac.uk/download/pdf/43539444.pdf

Tavares, Ana. *Dizes-me coisas amargas como os frutos*. Lisboa: Caminho, 2001.

___. *O Lago da Lua*. Lisboa: Caminho,1999.

___. "O Mirangolo' in Antologia da poesia feminina dos PALOP." Garcia X. L.(ed), Santiago de Compostela: Edicións Laiovento, 1998.

Chapter 4

Post-Colonial Identities on the Big Screen: Guinea-Bissau and São Tomé and Príncipe

Dr. Joseph Abraham Levi

George Washington University

Abstract

First, I will introduce some of the early literary records of Cape Verde,[1] Guinea-Bissau, and São Tomé and Príncipe as a way of opening the door to the "big screen" productions in and about these countries. This is necessary in order to understand the cultural and sociopolitical background against which Lusophone cinema came to be. I then address a springboard recent film productions such as *Luta ca caba inda* (Guinea-Bissau, Portuguese-based Creole[2] for "The Struggle is not Over Yet," 2012), *Spell Reel* (2018), and the trilogy *Viagem sem Volta 1*, *Viagem sem Volta 2*, and *Viagem sem Volta 3* (Ones-Way Trip 1, One-Way Trip 2, and One-Way Trip 3, 2017-2019), the first two film productions produced in Guinea-Bissau, whereas the last three hailing from São Tomé and Príncipe. In this study I will analyze how, despite the many difficulties in producing these motion pictures, at times mere home-made productions with improvised acting and make-shift studio equipment, European and African film producers living in Lusophone Africa have managed to convey the very essence of these African societies. In doing so they provide the audience with new insights on how to view and interpret the postcolonial

---

[1] Even though I will not address Cape Verdean films, the history of colonial Guinea-Bissau (1446-1974) and Cape Verde (1460-1974), the first six years of independence of Guinea-Bissau (declared: September 24, 1973; recognized: September 10, 1974), and the first five years of independence of Cape Verde (July 5, 1975) are inexorably intertwined. Cf. Joseph Abraham Levi. "Cabo Verde e São Tomé: Divergências e semelhanças literárias." *Mentalities/Mentalités* 18.2 (2004): 15-25.

[2] The word Creole comes from the Portuguese *Crioulo* (he/she who is being raised at home within a bilingual/bicultural environment), i.e., an offspring of a European (Portuguese) man and an indigenous woman, "raised" in both cultures. There are more than fifteen Portuguese-based Creoles spoken in the world, from Cape Verde and Guinea-Bissau to Macau (China) and Jakarta (Indonesia).

identity and multifaceted realities of Guinea-Bissau and São Tomé and Príncipe.

Keywords: Africa, Angola, cinema, documentaries, film, identity, independence, Lusophone, Portuguese, São Tomé and Príncipe

* * *

Lusophone Africa: First Literary Records

Since 1446, when the first Portuguese arrived in present-day Guinea-Bissau, until its independence, or rather, "[...] tanto antes como depois da sua independência em 1974, a história política e social da Guiné tem estado estreitamente ligada à de Cabo Verde"[3] (Hamilton 1984, 215). The first study on Guinea-Bissau was in fact written by a Cape Verdean – the merchant, chronicler, and captain André Álvares Gonçalves de Almada (Santiago, Cape Verde, sixteenth century) who wrote the *Tratado breve dos Rios de Guiné do Cabo-Verde* (Short Treatise of the Rivers of Cape Verde Guinea, 1594)[4] – whose work, notwithstanding the historical period in which it was written, contains a few attacks against the system, highlighting, within its limits, as well as what he was allowed to say by the Portuguese Crown, the local African cultures and societies:

> [...] a importância da descrição de Almada, a meu ver, deve ser a leitura que se faz da sociedade africana que cria mecanismos para se defender do poder, e combater as suas formas discricionárias e centralizadoras, tentando, de uma forma extremamente interessante, combater as suas "vertigens."[5] (Ferreira 1977, 89-90)

---

[3] "[...] either before or after its independence in 1974, the political and social history of Guinea-Bissau has been tightly linked to that one of Cape Verde." [translation provided by the author]

[4] For more information, see: André Álvares Gonçalves de Almada. *Relação e Descrição da Guiné, na Qual se Trata de Várias Nações de Negros Que a Povoam, dos Seus Costumes, Leis, Ritos, Cerimonias, Trajos, da Qualidade dos Portos e do Comércio Que neles Se Faz. Escreveu o Capitão André Gonçalves de Almada*; André Álvares Gonçalves de Almada. *Tratado Breve dos Rios da Guiné do Cabo-Verde*. 1594. Ed. António Luís Ferronha. Lisbon: Comissão Nacional para as Comemorações dos Descobrimentos Portugueses, 1994.

[5] "[...] the importance of Almada's description, in my view, should be his reading of African society, one that creates mechanisms for defending itself from power while fighting its discretionary and centralized forms, thus trying, in a very interesting way, to fight its "vertigos"." [translation provided by the author] (Almada 1994, 5).

However, we would have to wait until 1879 for the creation of the first printing press in Portuguese Guinea, a year later followed by the publication of the first local gazette, the *Boletim Oficial da Guiné*, (Guinea Official Bulletin), published for more than ninety years, namely, until 1974.[6]

As in other Portuguese-language literatures of the future Lusophone African countries, also in Guinea-Bissau,[7] the first literary works – from 1886 to almost the first half of the twentieth century – were of colonial nature where the people and the land are narrated by Portuguese or assimilated/*Portuguesized* native people. Incidentally, this feature remained until Guinea-Bissau ultimately gained its independence. In fact, "[…] até antes da independência nacional não foi possível ultrapassar a fase da literatura colonial. E esta mesmo de reduzida extensão."[8] In other words, given the sociopolitical obstacles, which hindered the birth and the flourishing of all art forms, "[…] durante a dominação portuguesa, não veio um poeta ou um romancista de mérito"[9] (Ferreira 1977, 89-90).

I

For a little over forty-six years, Portugal was under a stern military dictatorship, also referred to as *Estado Novo* (New State, 1926; 1928-1968), first with the fascist regime of António de Oliveira Salazar (1889-1970), and then (1968-1974) with his political heir and follower, Marcelo Caetano (1906-1980). Both dictators believed in maintaining and strengthening Portuguese presence in the country's overseas territories, provinces, enclaves, and colonies, particularly in Africa.

---

[6] *Boletim official do Governo da Provincia da Guiné Portugueza* (1884-1892); *Boletim official da Guiné Portugueza* (1892-1898); *Boletim official da Provincia da Guiné Portuguesa* (1898-1927); *Boletim oficial da Colónia da Guiné* (1927-1951); *Boletim oficial da Guiné* (1951-1974); *Boletim oficial* (1974-). Bolama (1884-1951); Bissau (1951-): Imprensa Nacional.

[7] Guinea-Bissau is divided in eight regions and an autonomous area, namely: Biombo (capital: Quinhamel), the autonomous area of Bissau (capital: Bissau), Bafatá (capital: Bafatá), Bolama (capital: Bolama), Cacheu (capital: Cacheu), Gabú (capital: Gabú), Oio (capital: Farim), Quinara (capital: Quinara), and Tombali (capital: Catió).

[8] "[…] until even before national independence it was not possible to overcome the colonial-literature phase, which was already minimal in its production." [translation provided by the author].

[9] "[…] during Portuguese domination, there were no poets or novelists of merit." [translation provided by the author].

Even though resistance began quite early in Cape Verde and Guinea-Bissau[10] – in some cases as early as the last decades of the nineteenth century – the last ten years of Salazar's regime (1958-1968) as well as Caetano's six-year reign of terror (1968-1974) saw the bulk of anti-colonial unrest and fight for independence in Portuguese Africa and Asia (East Timor). As for Portuguese Africa, Portuguese as well as African dissidents, all of leftist persuasion, with the former assisting the latter in building nationalist movements of Lusophone Africa, were usually sent to Cape-Verdean prisons, infamous for their brutal conditions (e.g., Tarrafal). Until the Lusophone African colonies officially gained independence (1975), anti-colonial insurgencies were the norm in Guinea-Bissau and, to a lesser degree, in the Archipelago of Cape Verde.[11]

The middle of the nineteenth century is usually considered as a ground-breaking point in the Lusophone African literary scene. The various printing presses that appeared in Cape Verde (1842), Angola (1845), Mozambique (1854), and São Tomé and Príncipe (1857) were the first steps towards an African and Portuguese-Creole presence, though limited and rigorously checked by the regime, within the Portuguese-speaking world.[12] While still in the hands of the Portuguese and/or of the Europeanized Creoles at the service of the colonial rule, the printing presses were in a sense the first examples of a Lusophone literary means of expression, one through which authors could express their identity and culture. Sadly enough, the indigenous African and/or Portuguese-based, Creole literary components were often seen and interpreted as cultural and anthropological "footnotes" rather than being viewed as free and legitimate literary expressions of the Lusophone-African world. This was especially the case of the *Boletins Oficiais* (Official Bulletins) that were also being printed in Portuguese Africa.

Also during the second half of the nineteenth century, the many *Almanaques* (Almanacs) which, though printed in Lisbon, hence froth with fascist and colonial propaganda, were exclusively dedicated to Luso-Brazilian and/or Lusophone African topics, were perhaps the first publications that offered literary pieces written by authors from all over the Portuguese-speaking world,

---

[10] During the last two decades of the nineteenth century, as well as after the 1884-1885 Berlin Conferences which, in a sense, officially started the so-called "Scramble for Africa," Cape Verde and Guinea-Bissau were the scene of the first oppositions to Portuguese rule in Africa. In 1886, the Portuguese Crown was indeed forced to send troops to suppress the incipient, anti-colonial unrest. It was not until the mid 1910s that the Portuguese troops were able to finally subdue the uprising in Guinea-Bissau.

[11] In 1956, the *Partido Africano para a Independência de Cabo Verde e da Guiné-Bissau* (PAICG) was formed.

[12] In Guinea-Bissau, the printing press appeared a few decades later than in its fellow Lusophone African territories/colonies, namely, in 1879.

from Lusophone Africa and Portuguese India to Macau and East Timor. Among the literary genres poetry, short stories, and novels that depict the daily life of everyday people stand out, as in the case of the Bantu-speaking population of Angola.[13]

II

[...] there is no denying that the [then] five [Lusophone] states do have a partially shared experience, based on a heritage of Portuguese influence and that, [more than] four decades ago, the nature of that influence transformed forever with independence. (Rothwell & Martinho 2016, 3)

The Colonial Wars in Portuguese Africa and Asia (East Timor) lasted roughly thirteen years (1961-1974).[14] Things changed after the fall of the dictatorial regime in Portugal (April 25, 1974), the democratization of Portugal, and the subsequent independence of the former Portuguese colonies in Africa (1975). Macau was returned to China on December 20, 1999, thus becoming China's second Special Administrative Region (1999-2049). East Timor became independent on May 20, 2002, since on December 7, 1975, it was unilaterally annexed by Indonesia at a time when it was still negotiating independence from Portugal (Levi 2020, 282). Obviously, for the future of the then-five African countries that later chose Portuguese as their official language,[15] these were the first steps towards the long journey for self-determination and complete independence from Portugal (1975). Though composed by Africans, the literary genres and topics found in these journals reflect a frame of mind that is typically European, in this case Portuguese. In a sense, the tone reflected an

---

[13] For further information on this topic, please see: Gerald Moser. *Almanach de Lembranças, 1854-1932*. Linda-a-Velha: ALAC-África, Literatura, Arte, Cultura, 1993.

[14] On July 31, 1961, the fort of São João Baptista de Ajudá was annexed by Benin (known as Dahomey until November 30, 1975). On December 18-19, 1961, Portuguese India (1501-1961) was annexed by India.

[15] On July 23, 2014, Equatorial Guinea—once a Portuguese colony and then, given to Spain by Portugal in exchange for more land in Brazil (Treaty of Saint Ildefonso, 1777, and Treaty of Pardo, 1778)—joined the CPLP (*Comunidade de Países de Língua Oficial Portuguesa*, Community of Countries whose Official Language is Portuguese). <https://www.cplp.org/>. Joseph Abraham Levi. "Intérpretes, escravos e almas necessitadas. Os africanos no espaço luso-atlântico dos primórdios," in *Senhores e Escravos nas Sociedades Ibero-Atlânticas*. Eds. Maria do Rosário Pimentel, and Maria do Rosário Monteiro. Lisbon: CHAM, Centro de Umanidades, Faculdade de Ciências Sociais e Humanas da Universidade NOVA de Lisboa, Universidade dos Açores, 2019 [2020]. 209-226. 212.

"appreciation of a classical Portuguese literary tradition" (Burness 1979, 183). While portraying a deep love for their land, their works – either written in Portuguese and/or in the different Portuguese-based Creoles spoken in Cape Verde, Guinea-Bissau, and São Tomé and Príncipe – in a sense continued to be manifestations of the Portuguese Empire, more precisely, they were part of Portuguese regionalism rather than being part of an indigenous, autonomous, and independent literary canon (Lopes 1988, ix).

However, this experience was fundamental for many Lusophone-African authors who already felt at ease with the African world and who, consequently, felt African. They were thus ready to delve into the rich and variegated indigenous African languages, cultures, and societies. They were ready to start a new literary genre within Portuguese and Brazilian letters, namely, Lusophone-African literature written in Portuguese and/or Portuguese-based Creole. In other words, it was the: "[...] regresso às fontes africanas, o estudo dos heróis negros [...] a propaganda de protesto, o tratamento de termos populares [...] uma auto-realização negra mais sincera e profunda" (Laranjeira 2000, xvi).

The historic and political context in which Lusophone Negritude came about did not allow the creation of a well-organized movement where people could express their ideas and goals freely, first and foremost independence from Portugal. Between 1949 and 1965, Salazar's fascist regime in fact intensified its oppressive methods. Francophone Negritude and the Harlem Renaissance that preceded it by seventeen years [16] were thus absorbed, transformed, and adapted to fit the needs of the Lusophone-African population living under the colonial regime. The Harlem Renaissance was in a sense instrumental for laying the groundwork, for instilling concepts such as human and equal rights, citizenship, free access to education, Black consciousness/pride, and equal opportunity. In a word, it was the birth of the "New Negro," or, as Léon Gontran Damas (1912-1978), a French writer from French Guiana, rightly said regarding his found sense of Negritude, it was "me sentir moi-même," i.e., "feeling myself" (Damas 1937, 5) for the first time ever.

The first Lusophone-African student of American literature was Francisco José de Vasques Tenreiro (1921-1963) who, though originally from São Tomé and Príncipe, spent almost all of his entire life in Portugal. [17] Incidentally,

---

[16] Particularly the third phase (mid 1926-1935), hence being concurrent to its birth (1934).

[17] Among Francisco Tenreiro's works, worth mentioning are: *Ilha de Nome Santo* (1942), *Contos e Poemas de Vários Autores Modernos Portugueses*, co-authored with Carlos Alberto Lança (1942), *Poesia Negra de Expressão Portu*guesa, co-authored with Brazilian Modernist Mário de Andrade (1953), *S. Tomé* (1961), *Obra Poética de Francisco José Tenreiro* (1967), and *Coração em África* (1977), the latter two published posthumously.

Tenreiro was the first Portuguese-speaking African writer who openly talked and wrote about Lusophone Negritude:

> Celle-ci sa poésie ne peut se constituer que dans un rapport continuel et passionné avec l'Afrique, avec son île natale, et avec les populations Africaines dispersés partout [...] Du point de vue poétique — confirmé par son écriture scientifique — Tenreiro ne prend jamais en charge les formes existentielles portugaises. Son discours symbolique ne peut s'organiser que dans le rapport avec les problèmes de l'Afrique, ou des Africaines, qu'ils soient des purs Africains, qu'ils soient des Afro-américains ou des Afro-brésiliens.[18] (Margarido 1985, 431)

In 1953, Mário Pinto de Andrade (Angola: 1928-1990) and Francisco José de Vasques Tenreiro published *Poesia negra de expressão portuguesa* (Black Poetry in Portuguese), in which they officially and openly vindicated Negritude. Though small in size, as well as in the number of copies available to the general public – usually limited to Lusophone-African students studying abroad – this text was instrumental in raising a new consciousness, namely, the *Negritude Africana de Língua Portuguesa*, i.e., Lusophone Negritude, among Lusophone-Africans throughout the world (Laranjeira 2000, xv).

Lusophone Africa: Literary Canon, Politics, War(s), and the Big Screen

"Throughout Portuguese-speaking Africa, film has become a medium of critique and re-evaluation of the independence era." (Rothwell and Martinho 2016, 60)

As Phillip Rothwell eloquently stated above, Lusophone African film productions tend to be reflections on and reevaluations of how they have adjusted to their much longed-for independence. Indeed, this is also true for most of Africa, particularly Sub-Saharan Africa where civil wars and civil unrest have been a constant for more than a decade in most cases. Additionally, and more importantly, the Cold War (1947-1991) had its repercussions in Africa, during and after the colonial wars (1954-1974), thus shifting the conflict

---

[18] "His poetry can only be composed within a continuous and passionate connection with Africa, with his native island, and with the African people dispersed throughout the world [...]. From a poetic point of view—confirmed by his scientific writings—Tenreiro never employs the Portuguese existential forms. His symbolic discourses are perforce organized around problems that concern Africa or Africans, Africans, as well as Afro-Americans, and Afro-Brazilians."

between the Iron Curtain (1945-1991) and its allies on one side, and the West on the other:

> Muitos países africanos ainda sofreram veementemente com guerras, guerrilhas e milícias que ocorreram sob influência de partidos políticos, declaradamente moldados de acordo com os interesses norte-americanos e soviéticos, marcados e fortalecidos após a 2ª Guerra Mundial.[19] (Chaves 2017, 34)

In other words, during the African colonial wars most African guerrilla fighters were supported by Communist countries like Cuba and the former Eastern Bloc, the latter led by the former USSR. Indeed, during the civil wars in Angola, Guinea-Bissau, and Mozambique, for example, there were political parties that aligned themselves either with the West or with the socialist and communist world:

> Realizadores e ativistas da França, da Iugoslávia, de Cuba e da União Soviética aderiram à produção do cinema nesses países, concentrando seus esforços e talentos em visões emancipatórias, a favor dos movimentos de libertação. Logo, o filme foi desenvolvido como uma ferramenta ideológica estratégica para documentar, educar e disseminar, tanto para o povo africano quanto para a comunidade internacional, informações sobre as guerras anticoloniais e sobre a condição histórica do povo africano.[20] (Arenas 2011, 37)

Perhaps another reason for seeking alliances with these countries is the fact that, unlike Belgian, British, and French colonial rules in Africa, the Portuguese regime, particularly during the last fourteen years of its existence (1960-1974), did not invest in encouraging a local, African film industry (Meleiro 2011, 137). Things changed with the fall of the Berlin Wall (November 9, 1989) and the end of the Communist strongholds around the world.

---

[19] ["Many African countries also had many wars, guerrillas, and militia that were influenced by political parties, clearly molded by American and Soviet interests, which only increased after the Second World War." [translated by the author].

[20] ["Film producers and activists hailing from France, [former] Yugoslavia, Cuba, and the [former] Soviet Union joined film productions in these [African] countries, concentrating their efforts and talents in emancipation visions, and favoring liberation movements. Hence, the film [industry] was developed as a strategic, ideological tool in order to educate and disseminate, among the African as well as the international community, information on anti-colonial wars and the historic conditions of the African people]. [translated by the author].

Indeed, African nations coming out of their civil wars, such as Angola, Guinea-Bissau, and Mozambique, had to negotiate their political views within this new political system that was more open to capitalist ventures in their countries; yet, for the most part, they remained unaffected and continued to rule as before: MPLA (*Movimento Popular de Libertação de Angola*, Popular Movement for the Liberation of Angola) in Angola, the PAIGC (*Partido Africano da Independência da Guiné-Bissau e Cabo Verde*, African Party for the Independence of Guinea-Bissau and Cape Verde) in Guinea-Bissau, and FRELIMO (*Frente de Libertação de Moçambique*, Liberation Front for Mozambique) in Mozambique, all continued along with their leftist views, though now forging new ties with capitalist countries. Unfortunately, the elite in power shared the profits of these economic changes, not the rest of the population which continued to live below the poverty level.

Furthermore, and whenever possible, these political parties "involved in the liberation struggles" in Angola, Cape Verde and Guinea-Bissau, and Mozambique, "invited international filmmakers" from the West (e.g., France) and the Socialist/Communist countries mentioned above, "to accompany their wars of independence" (Ferreira 2011, 222) against the Portuguese. It was their way to record the events for posterity as they were happening. It was their way to reflect upon the impact of these wars on their lives as they were forging a new nation and negotiating a new national identity.

The movie industry in post-civil war Lusophone Africa reflects this dichotomy whereby the interest is in either rediscovering their colonial past or in reexamining and shedding some light on the reasons why – despite the rich natural resources of their countries, increased foreign capital investments and aid from the West as well as from China, the latter a major investor whose real intentions in Africa are reasons for concern – things have not improved socioeconomically since independence. Indeed, the new generation of Lusophone Africans is disillusioned with the powers-that-be and their kleptocracy:

> [...] their rulers are not heroes who defeated the Portuguese and gave birth to new nations, but politicians who in some cases have been in power for a very long time. The cultural sphere of the young is increasingly a space where the "nation" is contested rather than "forged," as was the case during the early years following independence. (Phyllis Peres in Rothwell and Martinho 2016, 3)

This explains why most Lusophone African film productions fall under the category of documentary or reflections on the colonial and civil war periods, as a way of understanding the past while, at the same time, rejecting and fighting the corruption of their leaders.

> The Portuguese-speaking countries of Africa (Angola, Mozambique, Cape Verde, Guinea-Bissau, and São Tomé [and Príncipe]) [...] have been unable to sustain film productions, and their emerging cinematographers are still dominated by documentaries. There is little or no fiction film. (João Paulo Carlos Rodrigues in Roof 2004, 258)

Obviously, this leaves little room for anything else. Of course, there are exceptions whereby genres such as romance, mental health, and horror, for example, are being explored by young Lusophone African and/or Westerners film producers living and working in Lusophone Africa.

On April 23, 2019, members of the jury of the First Edition of the *Prémio António Loja Neves* (António Loja Neves Prize), instituted by the *Federação Portuguesa de Cineclubes* (Portuguese Federation of Film Clubs), (*Federação Portuguesa de Cineclubes*) a Portuguese foundation created to honor the late Portuguese journalist and film director António Loja Neves (1953-2018), narrowed their choice among more than fifty entries to six Lusophone African films for a non-monetary, biannual prize aimed at "promoting and awarding cinematography hailing from Lusophone Africa" (Seis Filmes da África Lusófona Nomeados).

These six films represented Guinea-Bissau ("Arriaga," by Welket Bungué (1980-)), Mozambique ("Comboio de Sal e Açúcar," Salt and Sugar Train, by Brazilian-born, Mozambican resident Licínio Azevedo (1951-), and "Mabata Bata," by Sol de Carvalho (Mozambique: 1953-)), Cape Verde ("Homestay," by Loló Arziki (1992-)), and São Tomé and Príncipe ("O Canto do Ossobó," The Song of the Ossobó, by Silas Tiny (1982-), and "Sonho Longínquo no Equador," "Faraway Dream at the Equator," by Hamilton Leite Ramos da Trindade (1983-)). The winner was the Mozambican film "Mabata Bata" (2017), loosely based on the short story "O dia em que explodiu Mabata Bata" (The Day Mabata Bata Exploded), contained in Mia Couto's 1968 short stories collection *Vozes Anoitecidas* (Voices Made Night).[21]

Yet, most African film productions are not known in the West, except for rare apparitions at international film festivals. Hence, when they do appear in the West, very little information is found on their producers:

---

[21] Mia Couto (1955-), penname of António Emílio Leite Couto, acclaimed Mozambican writer. Cf. Joseph Abraham Levi, ed. *Contemporary Literary Criticism: Mia Couto.* Columbia, SC: Gale Cengage, 2015.

[...] conhecer o cinema africano exige algum esforço. Os filmes são pouco divulgados, muitas exibições ficam restritas a poucos e esporádicos festivais de cinema, de forma que muitos apreciadores e estudiosos restam quase impossibilitados de conhecer essas produções.[22] (Chaves 2017, 34)

Most importantly though, actually almost always, very little can be found on the creative processes behind these bourgeoning film productions. Hence, in order to overcome these obstacles, it is imperative to follow the cultural and geopolitical affiliation, or reaction to, of these African or African-based film producers:

Para conhecer as narrativas fílmicas, é imprescindível pesquisar a trajetória dos cineastas e conhecer o contexto histórico e geopolítico de quando esses filmes foram feitos. Mas o esforço para empreender esta busca e ter contato com este cinema é recompensado por obras fílmicas admiráveis, que se revelam muito interessantes, inovadoras e dotadas de altíssima qualidade artística. Conhecer este cinema, além de ser uma oportunidade de ver bons filmes, é uma forma de compreender melhor o universo cultural e intercultural dessas nações.[23] (Chaves 2017, 34)

Guinea-Bissau: *Luta ca caba inda* (2012) and *Spell Reel* (2018)

From their screening in isolated villages in Guinea-Bissau to European capitals, the silent reels are now a place from which people may search for antidotes to a world in crisis.[24]

---

[22] "[...] knowing African cinema requires some efforts. [African] films are not distributed [overseas]; many viewings are restricted to a few and sporadic film festivals; hence, many [foreign] film aficionados and scholars have no chance of knowing these films." [translated by the author].

[23] ["In order to understand the narrative of these films it is imperative to study the trajectory of the film producers and understand the historic and geopolitical context of when these films were produced. Yet, this effort in getting to know [African] cinema is compensated by wonderful films that are very interesting, innovative, and with a high artistic value. Getting to know this cinema, besides being an opportunity of seeing good films, it is a way of better understanding the cultural and intercultural universe of these nations. " [translated by the author].

[24] "13 – 20.04.2018 screenings, display and books launch *Spell Reel Luta ca caba inda* & The struggle is not yet over." *Archive Kabinett* April 13, 2018. <http://www.archivekabinett. org/product/13-20-04-2018-screenings-display-and-books-launch-spell-reel-luta-ca-caba-inda-the-struggle-is-not-over-yet/>.

Filipa César (1975-) is a Portuguese artist who lives and works in Berlin. She holds a degree in Fine Arts (Painting) from Lisbon (1999), has studied at the Academy of Arts in Munich (1999-2000), has had an internship at the Arri-TV, Munich (Production, Cinematography, Montage, and Post-Production, 2000-2001), was a visiting filmmaker at the HFF Konrad Wolf, Potsdam (2005-2006), holds an MA in Art from the Berlin University of Arts (MA Art in Context, 2008), and is currently a PhD candidate at the FCSH-New University, Lisbon. Her fields are Photography and Time-Based Media (e.g., videos, documentaries, and films).

Filipa César has exhibited her work at the Istanbul Biennial (2003), the Kunsthall Wien (2004), the Serralves Museum in Porto (2005), the Locarno International Film Festival, Switzerland (2005), the CAG-Contemporary Art Gallery, Vancouver (2006), the Tate Modern (2007), the St. Gallen Museum, Switzerland (2007), the Prague International Triennale of Contemporary Art festival (2008), the SF MOMA, San Francisco (2009), the 12th Architecture Biennial, Venice (2010), the 29th São Paulo Biennial (2010), the 2010 Mostra Internacional de Cinema de São Paulo (São Paulo International Film Festival) ("Filipa César." *MUBI*), and the Manisfesta 8 film festival (Murcia and Cartagena, Spain, October 9, 2010-January 9, 2011).

Filipa César's ties with Guinea-Bissau go back to 2008 when, while talking to Bissau-Guinean poet, playwright, and stage director, Carlos Vaz (1954-) – then president of the Guinea-Bissau *Instituto do Cinema* (National Institute of Cinema, INC in the Portuguese acronym), created in Bissau in 1977 – she became aware that there were many, not catalogued, and severely damaged audiovisual records of the Portuguese Colonial War (1961-1974) somewhere stored in Bissau:

> They showed me a room full of film canisters in a very wet and gloomy environment at the Institute of Cinema in Bissau. N'Hada told me that this was where their early work as the first Guinean filmmakers was stored, and how he, at the age of seventeen had been picked out from the middle of the jungle war and sent by Amílcar Cabral to Cuba to become a filmmaker — and how he had never seen a film before. (César 2016)

That was the beginning of many years of research and editing, since some of the reels were in an advanced stage of deterioration due to weather conditions as well as sociopolitical events that occurred in Guinea-Bissau. Eventually, in 2012, "moved [...] by the imminent loss of the archive," (César 2016) Filipa César was able to digitalize most of the material found in Bissau (Brunel 2013). Her desire was to continue what was never completed, or rather, show "a militant cinema of emancipation, born from the struggle as a praxis of liberation and a possible deviation from [her] own imagery" (César 2016).

The footage was eventually restored at the *Arsenal – Institut für Film und Videokunst e.V.* (Institute for Film and Video Art E.V.) in Berlin, with the assistance of an "'alliance' that [...] brought together Guinean and European artists, filmmakers, and researchers [in order to save] the country's cinematic memory through a [...] process of digitalization and premastering" (Cardina 2019).

On December 1, 2012, Filipa César, together with Bissau-Guinean screenwriters and film directors Sana na N'Hada (1950-) and Flora Gomes (1949-), presented the documentary *Luta ca caba inda* (Guinea-Bissau, Portuguese-based Creole for "The Struggle is Not Over Yet") which bears the same title as "an unfinished project that began at INC in 1980" aiming at recording "Guinea-Bissau's six years after independence" (Cardina 2019).

Interestingly enough, Filipa César used parts of the title to coauthor a book on this topic, namely, *Luta ca caba inda: time place matter voice. 1967-2017*, whereby many unfinished or never-before, displayed articles are for the first time brought to light, thus representing the "written record of a process of rescue and re-reading" (Cardina 2019).

Luta ca caba inda: time place matter voice. 1967-2017 is a book made of "fragments: testimonial excerpts, stills, unfinished film records, reports, and book covers about the struggle." Indeed, the emphasis of her work is on the fragments, since they stress the "precariousness of the archives" in which they were found while, at the same time, they point out at the "subject historical vicissitudes and to the corrosiveness of time," thus resembling «an assemblage of shrapnel»" (Cardina 2019). Additionally, its "dialogues and discussions between different protagonists (between 2010 and 2017) intersect with visual documents about the struggle and the subsequent process of nation building" (Cardina 2019).

Ironically, though, the timeframe of the book gives life and eternity to names and events that otherwise would have forever been forgotten: "The time it engages with comes alive to the exact extent that its ruined dimension requires carefully recovering existing fragments and, at the same time, undertaking an hermeneutic exercise that makes them visible and contemporary" (Cardina 2019).

German writer, video programmer, exhibitions editor, and independent film curator Tobias Hering (1971-) also introduced the work which took place in Paris at the *Jeu de Paume Museum*, in collaboration with the *Berlin Arsenal – Institut für Film und Videokunst e.V.* Furthermore, between October 16, 2012, and January 20, 2013, the *Jeu de Paume Museum* featured an art show curated by Paris-based, Portuguese freelancer Filipa Oliveira (1974-), also titled *Luta ca caba inda*, and part of the *Satellite 5 (Jeu de Paume 2012)* show, where Filipa César shared visual background information and material that led to the creation of the documentary, like photographs, printed documents, and information on "her father's military service in Portuguese Guinea" (Brunel 2013). Indeed, yet indirectly and perhaps subconsciously, Filipa César's father was instrumental in her awakening to rediscovering her ties with Guinea-Bissau:

> My father was the channel, after his failed desertion to Paris, he had served in the military in Portuguese Guinea between 1967 and 1969. I was introduced to an imagery of resistance to Salazar's regime — underground subversive political literature, the illegal emigration of deserters and political activists and a revolution through the radio transmission of coded song. (César 2016)

In the documentary *Luta ca caba inda*, Filipa César introduces the audience to her work as she went through all the scattered and ill-conserved material on and about the War of Liberation against Portugal fought in Guinea-Bissau (1961-1974). The documentary was filmed in a single take, showing three people talking about the Portuguese Colonial War, particularly the parts highlighting the role of the main leader of the independence movement, or rather, Amílcar Lopes Cabral (1924-1973).

Intermingled with the war stories, there are also discussions on the history of Bissau-Guinean cinema. The first two people in this discussion are assistant director Suleimane Biai (1968-) and Carlos Vaz, who were chosen because of their active role in the Bissau-Guinean guerrilla war against Portuguese rule in Lusophone Africa, particularly in Cape Verde and Guinea-Bissau. The third person in the film is Joanna Barrios, Filipa César's alter ego if you will.

As Filipa César later mentioned, "*Luta ca caba inda* showed itself to us as an irrelevant irreverent force that claims: I am not from yesterday. It is a projectile that is traveling for decades, centuries, and offered the chance to join the journey." Indeed, "*Luta ca caba inda* produced an inversion too — the archive started to grow instead of shrink" (César 2016). The main focus of the *Luta ca caba inda* is Amílcar Cabral's life and his efforts to defeat Portuguese oppression in Cape Verde and Guinea-Bissau. Interestingly, the documentary also highlights Cabral's decision to send in 1966 four young Bissau-Guineans, namely, Flora Gomes, Sana na N'Hada, Josefina Crato, and José Bolama Cobumba "to the Cuban Film Institute (ICAIC) to learn how to make cinema" (Portuguese Artist Filipa César 2012). Indeed, Amílcar Cabral's purpose was that upon their return to Guinea-Bissau these guerrilla fighters could "film the struggle" (Cardina 2019) for independence of Cape Verde and Guinea-Bissau from Portugal. ICAIC was then led by renowned Cuban filmmaker Santiago Álvarez Román (1919-1998), famous for his "nervous montage" approach to filmmaking whereby he would mix images, photographs, and movie clips, including cartoons, to create a new product of "found materials" (César 2016).

Eventually, the four "Cuban-trained," Bissau-Guineans named above were able to document "their country's struggles" for independence "from 1963 to 1974." Yet, the footage was forgotten and improperly stored, only to be "recovered in 2001." Alas, "only about 40 of the original 100 hours of footage were salvageable" (Glessing 2018, 139).

During a conversation with Filipa César, Sana na N'Hada stated: "I've been very lucky, I've never had to point a gun at anyone. It's not that there weren't situations where I could have fired a gun, but I had a camera in my hand instead. And that is better" (Portuguese Artist Filipa César 2012). In fact, in 1966 these four Bissau-Guineans had to learn the latest techniques of the time in cinematography so that they could document the decolonization process in Guinea-Bissau (Martins 2019). This is because, for "Cabral, cinema was a way of" educating and uniting the more than "40 ethnic groups" so that they could "join the same aim – Independence" (César 2016). Indeed, the aim of this documentary is to highlight Amílcar Cabral's vision, or rather, to empower the new generation so that it can create a new, independent nation, Guinea-Bissau and Cape Verde. Cinema was seen as the best way to visually portray positive images of this new burgeoning country. Indeed, the vision then was to create one new nation: Cape Verde and Guinea-Bissau. Cinema was thus "a political tool, a way to create a new collective memory, to write [the] history of the new liberated Guinea[-Bissau and Cape Verde] with another empowered voice" (César 2016).

Thanks to Cabral, Bissau-Guinean cinema made its first appearance in Guinea-Bissau because of the talents of the recipients of these scholarships to Cuba. Unfortunately, the Bissau-Guinean Civil War (June 7, 1998-May 10, 1999) brought an end to this dream. Even though it was short-lived, the 1980 coup d'état and the bloody Bissau-Guinean Civil War left an everlasting destructive effect on the country: it destroyed the already frail infrastructure, thus damaging even further the local economy (Filipa César: 'Luta ca caba inda' 2012). Obviously, there were additional factors that contributed to the collapse of this burgeoning and promising cinema in Guinea-Bissau. As Carolin Overhoff Ferreira underscored, "civil wars, economic crises, corruption, the end of the cold war, and the general lack of funding, infrastructure, equipment, and qualified technicians, soon brought an end to these promising beginnings" (Ferreira 2011, 222) in Angola, Mozambique, and Guinea-Bissau.

As the three characters discuss Cabral's role images of *Guiné-Bissau 6 anos depois* (Guinea-Bissau 6 Years Later) – a never-released documentary made by Flora Gomes and Sana na N'Hada before the peaceful, 1980 military coup d'état that deposed the country's first Bissau-Guinean president Luís Cabral (1931-2009) – are "projected onto the stage, immersing the participants of the talk" (Brunel 2013).

This brilliant scenographic idea gives momentum to the entire dialog-conversation, since it offers the audience the impression that the hidden or forgotten history of Guinea-Bissau is now being relived, revitalized, and shown anew by words (those of the three characters) and images (the never-released documentary), thus empowering the living and those who died for their freedom.

The influence of renowned French documentary film-producer, photographer, and writer Chris Marker (1921-2012), one of the first westerners to produce anti-colonial documentaries and films, *Les statues meurent aussi* (Statues Also Die, 1953), is evident not only when it comes to denouncing colonial views of African life and artifacts, but also in the dichotomy of life and death: sacred African objects dead and/or lifeless in Europe (museums/private residences) vs. life/sacred objects conveying emotions and spirituality. It is important to stress here that inviting foreign filmmakers like Chris Marker to cooperate with film producers hailing from or living in Africa is a trait common to most postcolonial African countries, since the experience and expertise of these renowned masters of the big screen allow for dialogue and growth, both doors to the creation of (future) autochthonous productions. Indeed, while owing their existence to foreign intervention, these new productions produced in Africa are nevertheless a witness to a new consciousness and desire to explore *topoi* such as how to negotiate the colonial past with national characteristics and idiosyncrasies. In this documentary, Filipa César actually brings to life the dead, almost-forgotten, and almost lost-forever names and images of people who fought for their independence. This includes the abovementioned never-released documentary, since by showing it in the background Filipa César is giving it (new) life and, in a sense, (new) power: the power to tell a story that has been silenced by the colonial regime.

Interestingly enough, among the treasure-trove of images, photographs, and movie reels found abandoned in Bissau, Filipa César also stumbled upon "footages [...] some in editing process, few finished films, a collection of films from allied countries such as GDR, USSR, Cuba, and Sweden, as well as video copies of films left by Chris Marker" (Portuguese Artist Filipa César 2012). Indeed, the then Bissau-Guinean Minister of Culture, Mário Coelho Pinto de Andrade (1928-1990) invited Chris Marker to lead filmmaking workshops in Bissau. Chris Marker "would later integrate carnival footage shot by N'Hada into his 1983 documentary *Sans Soleil* [Without the Sun]," (MoMa Presents 2017) whereby the motif of human memory is questioned as it inevitably affects humanity and its perceived values. Even though some scenes were shot in Cape Verde, Iceland, Paris, and San Francisco, most of the images and scenes in *Sans Soleil* are from Guinea-Bissau and Japan which were purposely chosen by Chris Marker to show "two extreme poles of survival" (Rosenbaum 2007).

As for memory, "Filipa César's work shows how the cinema in Guinea-Bissau synthesizes archaeological vestiges, written documents and subjective memory" (Cardina 2019). In fact, six years after the debut of *Luta ca caba inda*, *Spell Reel* is finally released. Like its predecessor, the ninety-six minute film *Spell Reel* showcases Filipa César and her coauthors' intent to make the "past and its struggles resonate with those of today, through a polyphonic montage of stories and places" (Spell Reel. Filipa César 2020). In other words, *Spell Reel* is a multilayered and powerful work that:

> [...] charts the screening process and its potent mix of filmic and oral storytelling traditions, while noting the conditions of the material's initial creation—resulting in a complex portrait of a nation whose cinematic legacy helped shape its liberation. (Spell Reel NWFILM.ORG)

Moreover, like its predecessor, *Spell Reel* in Portuguese, Fula (Fulani), Guinea-Bissau Portuguese-based Creole, English, and French, with English subtitles – is a well-devised and weaved montage of images and dialogues with the aim of recovering the past by giving it a voice and memory as well as a present and a future:

> *Spell Reel* is not only an adventure about memory but also a powerful gesture of transmission and sharing in which this fragile political and artistic heritage of Guinean cinema finds universal and contemporary resonance. (Spell Reel. Filipa César 2020)

In order to fulfill their goals, Filipa César and her fellow filmmakers traveled to the places in Guinea-Bissau where the original footage was first shot and showed it to the locals, for the most part composed of "a generation largely ignorant of" (Kenigsberg 2017) the struggles of their forefathers. In a sense, the movie is showing people archives, making them alive in "makeshift screens," yet again, and it is asking for people to participate and to add their own commentaries:

> The first image is in black and white, upside down and projected into a black box that then becomes the frame. It now hovers like a time capsule near a man's face. He looks down, listening in on a female guerrilla

fighter and translating her words from Fulani. Within the capsule, money is counted and paid out as a new currency, the numbers of the years run backwards in the black box. A 16-mm film glides through the man's hands and is transferred to a laptop screen frame by frame (Spell Reel Cinept 2017). In fact, as "more and more people watch these old films, they become aware of a past they have been systematically denied" (Choudhury 2017).

Reflecting upon the fact that much of the footage from the period survives only as fragments, the film asks, What is restoration where there is no original to return to? In superbly vivid tableaux, the film juxtaposes the black-and-white 16mm footage with contemporary digital images, subtly manipulating scale, orientation, and text to alternatively create distance or achieve proximity between past and present. The film also documents the 2014 mobile cinema tour that introduced the digitized footage to Guinean audiences who were discovering a chapter in their history for the first time. N'Hada, Gomes, and others offered commentary during the screenings, positing that collective experience and oral history are intrinsic to the films' renewed life (MoMa Presents 2017).

It is clear then that the filmmakers' intent is to empower Bissau-Guineans as they bring to light on screen their own history and struggle. Hence, the story, or the overall plot if you will, is multifaceted, non-linear, never-ending, and ever-changing, "as it constantly juxtaposes and superimposes archival footage on the present." Indeed, its empty spaces leave "room for future narratives to come and fill in these gaps" (Choudhury 2017).

The ultimate goal, then, is not just to report and show "emotional invocations of" Bissau-Guineans for independence, but rather, to portray their "physical and sensory engagements with the history of" their Nation" (Choudhury 2017). In other words, *Spell Reel* gives them tools to take control of their own past while, at the same time, it encourages them to research and rediscover their past since knowledge is power:

> *Spell Reel* celebrates education, in the form of the mobile cinema tour, as avant-garde work, and César's ambition and finesse in recovering a fragile artistic and social history prove she is an inheritor of the tradition explored in her film: art that furthers intellectual and political ideals for all (MoMa Presents 2017).

As mentioned above, Amílcar Cabral's dream was to train young Bissau-Guineans in the art of filmmaking so that through their work they could help keep alive the struggles of a nation, then still in the making. Amílcar "Cabral's teaching methods" are in a sense reflected and perhaps continued in *Spell Reel* at least in its "avant-garde style" (Kenigsberg 2017) and approach to presenting the issue and offering possible solutions to the future generation to follow:

> The film, in its archaeological pursuit, is a fitting tribute to the legacy of Amílcar Cabral – the revolutionary who steered Guinea-Bissau's freedom struggle, and the agricultural engineer. Through its recurrent going back to imageries of earth, the soil and the trees, the film creates a knowledge system that can be seen and immediately related to. It evokes a sense of political empowerment that can only come from *seeing* for oneself and not being merely *taught* to see. In creating *Spell Reel*, its makers move a step closer to attaining the freedom that Cabral envisaged—a freedom attained through knowledge and fearlessness (Choudhury 2017).

III

> [...] São Tomé and Príncipe's insularity and relatively small population size [...] has shaped its development as a nation. Despite its strong historical links to Angola, through a colonial system of slavery and forced labor, São Tomé and Príncipe, like Cabo Verde, has often seen its island status as a source of isolation and difference, as well as creating a nexus linking it to a diaspora around the globe. (Rothwell and Martinho 2016, 2)

Even though they portray features found in other Lusophone- (particularly Cape Verdean) or pan-African literatures, São Tomé e Príncipe letters boast a unique body of work that sets it aside from most contemporary African nations, particularly Lusophone African countries, as in the case of Cape Verde and Guinea-Bissau.

The transatlantic exchanges that occurred between the fifteenth and the twentieth century also left a mark in the literary production of this young African nation. European settlement and colonization, Sephardic presence (Levi 2004, 1-25), transatlantic slavery, transcontinental Diasporas and (im)migrations – enforced, chosen, or self imposed – had all an effect on São Tomean literary genres and motifs, particularly short stories and theatrical representations (e.g., the Tchiloli) (Levi 2012, 349-368). Indeed, short stories, theatrical representations, and, as of late, motion pictures are the best examples of this encounter/mixing of cultures and languages.

Hence, the sociopolitical and economic experimentation(s) that occurred everywhere in the Atlantic world had, per force, a counterpart at the cultural level. São Tomean literature and cinema, in Portuguese and/or in any of its Portuguese-based Creoles spoken in the archipelago, are perhaps the keys to understanding the complex dynamics that—for almost six hundred years,[25] if we count the ties between Europe and Africa, or more than five hundred years if, on the other hand, we also include the Americas into the equation—have been attracting, repelling, and conjoining two/three continents and their people.

São Tomé and Príncipe

[...] Portugal set up official regulations for the funding of transnational films with Cape Verde in 1989, with Mozambique in 1990, with Angola in 1992, and with São Tomé and Príncipe in 1994. (Ferreira 2011, 222)

During colonial times, in São Tomé and Príncipe as well as the rest of the then Portuguese empire, the Portuguese Government was not keen to invest in filmmaking produced in and for its overseas possessions. Indeed, the first film productions were documentaries exploring the local flora, fauna, and the ethnography of the Portuguese lands outside Portugal. In a way, they served as political propaganda, reinforcing the needs of the regime to maintain its colonies, enclaves, and possessions in Africa and Asia because these territories and their people were prosperous thanks to Portuguese presence, past and present.

In 1908-1909, the documentary A *Cultura do Cacau em São Tomé* (Coco Bean Plantations in São Tomé) was produced by acclaimed Portuguese photographer and film producer Ernesto Januário Gualdino de Sousa Albuquerque (1883-1940) whereby coco bean plantations in São Tomé and Príncipe are shown for the first time on the big screen. Interestingly enough, images of forced labor were the producer's way of denouncing this immoral practice by the (in)famous multinational company Cadbury (McNeil 2016).

In 1909, Manuel Cardoso Furtado and José Soares Andrade directed and produced *O Cacau Escravo e o Trabalho Indígena em São Tomé* (Coco Bean Slaves and Indigenous Labor in São Tomé) which was shown at the *Exposition Universelle et Internationale de Bruxelles* (Brussels International Exposition,

---

[25] Modern Area interests in and occupation of other spaces outside Europe officially began in 1415 with the Portuguese siege of Ceuta—a Portuguese enclave in Morocco (1415-1580), then a Spanish town and seaport (1580-to the present). However, towards the end of the thirteenth century, and during the first decades of the fourteenth century, Portuguese navigators, with the aid of Genoese, Pisan, Catalan, and Majorcan sailors, were already exploring the Atlantic sea.

April 23-November 1, 1910). The digital archives[26] of the Universidade da Beira Interior in Covilhã, Portugal, indicate *A Vida nas Roças de São Tomé* (Life on São Tomé Plantations) yet another documentary produced by Furtado in 1909. Nevertheless, according to Maria do Carmo Piçarra, this is most likely only a different title for *Cacau Escravo e o Trabalho Indígena em São Tomé* (Piçarra 2016, 129). Also in 1909, Manuel Cardoso Furtado and José Soares Andrade produced *Serviçal e Senhor* (Servant and Master) also shown at the 1910, Brussels International Exposition.[27] Both films were projected in Tervueren, a Belgian municipality in the Flemish province of Brabant, which hosted all art forms that concentrated on the European colonies, enclaves, and territories overseas.[28]

Following independence, and despite the good intentions and the agreements/cooperation with European countries, like the one reported in the abovementioned quote, when it comes to São Tomé and Príncipe very little has been produced by, or with the assistance of, film producers hailing from this small archipelago in the Gulf of Guinea. Postcolonial filmmaking in São Tomé and Príncipe began more than two decades after its independence with the 1998 film *Früchtchen: Am Äquator ist alles möglich* (translated in Portuguese as *A frutinha do Equador*, i.e., The Little Fruit from the Equator) directed by the late Austrian film director and author Herbert Brodl (1949-2015). It was shown at the 1998, Nordische Filmtage Lübeck (Lübeck Nordic Film Days). The plot of this work – the first full-length film completely shot in São Tomé and Príncipe – is very captivating, almost foreshadowing the future trends of São Tomean likes on the big screen: i.e., an intriguing blend of comedy and fantasy, all based on São Tomé mores.

Alas, *Früchtchen: Am Äquator ist alles möglich* did not immediately set a trend, since the next seven films produced in São Tomé in cooperation with or by São Tomeans were documentaries focusing on the islands, and did not address the likes and dislikes of its people when it comes to the Seventh Art, namely: *Extra Bitter: The Legacy of the Chocolate Islands* (2000, directed by Canadian documentary connoisseur Derek Vertongen);[29] *São Tomé, cent-pour-cent cacao* (São Tomé, One-Hundred Percent Cocoa Beans, 2004, directed by renowned French director Virginie Berda); *Mionga ki Ôbo – Mar e Selva. Mer et*

---

[26] For more information see: "M. Cardoso Furtado." CINEPT – CINEMA PORTUGUÊS. http://www.cinept.ubi.pt/pt/pessoa/2143688896/M.+Cardoso+Furtado.

[27] For more information see: Guido Convents. "Portugal," in Richard Abel, ed. *Encyclopedia of Early Cinema*. London: Routledge, 2012. 527-528.

[28] For more information see: "Expo 1919 Brussels." *Bureau International des Expositions.* <https://www.bie-paris.org/site/en/1910-brussels>.

[29] Library. Deakin University. <http://library.deakin.edu.au/record=b3425127>.

forêt (Miongo ki Ôbo - Sea and Jungle, 2005, directed by Equatorial-Guinean born, São Tomean actor Ângelo Torres); *The Lost Wave* (2007, directed by prominent American director, screenwriter, and surfer Sam George); the documentary *Tchiloli – Identidade de um Povo* (Tchiloli – Identity of a Nation, 2010), directed by the São Tomeans Felisberto Branco and Kalú Mendes; *Água boa, vida saudável* (Good Water, Healthy Life, 2011), produced by Kalú Mendes and financed by the International Red Cross; and the documentary *Ilha do Príncipe – o Éden Esquecido do Atlântico* (The Island of Príncipe – The Forgotten Eden of the Atlantic, 2014), produced by the Portuguese João Teles de Vasconcelos and sponsored by a Portuguese NGO, aidnature.org.[30]

São Tomé and Príncipe:
Viagem sem Volta 1, Viagem sem Volta 2, Viagem sem Volta 3
(One-Way Trip 1, One-Way Trip 2, One-Way Trip 3, 2017-2019)

A produção em São Tomé e Príncipe é quase inexistente. […] Há também filmes que relatam alguns episódios ocorridos no país […] (Chaves 2017, 42).[31]

Alas, almost two decades would have to pass until a group of young São Tomeans has the opportunity to create something that addresses the needs of their people: fantasy, the macabre, and horror on the big screen. This trend began around the early years of the first decade of the twenty-first century; yet, it was only in 2017 that things materialized thanks to the vision, determination, and fearless entrepreneurship of young São Tomean men.

Viagem sem Volta 1, Viagem sem Volta 2, and *Viagem sem Volta 3* are part of a horror-movie trilogy produced in and by young men and women from São Tomé and Príncipe between 2017 and 2019. The two men behind these projects are Mr. Aguinaldo Penhor and Mr. Dodamy Lift. During a telephone conversation with Mr. Penhor,[32] I was informed that in 2014 Mr. Penhor and Mr. Lift had a dream: creating a film company, *Mudaico Filmes*. Unfortunately, Mr. Penhor and Mr. Lift had no financial backing and had to use their own funds to spearhead and continue with their project.

Mudaico is a Portuguese neologism for *Mudar* (to change) + *companhia* (company), or rather, "a company" that wants to "change" the world. In other words, the desire of these two young, São Tomean men was to create a business

---

[30] Aidnature.org. <https://www.linkedin.com/company/aidnature-org/about/>.
[31] "The production in São Tomé and Príncipe is almost inexistent. […] There are also films that narrate some episodes that have occurred in the country." [translated by the author].
[32] May 25, 2020.

dedicated to producing films featuring São Tomé and Príncipe, its people, and its mores. Due to the fact that at that time there was not a film industry created and run by people from São Tomé and Príncipe, in 2014 *Mudaico Filmes* was formed with the aim of developing and incentivizing the production of original movies in the country. Its goal is to promote São Tomean culture at home and abroad. Indeed, throughout our telephone conversation, Mr. Penhor urged me to convey this message: "Please make sure that your readers know what we are doing and that they view and eventually purchase our films."

For Mr. Penhor and Mr. Lift, producing eerie and slightly-macabre films was the best way of promoting São Tomé and Príncipe. According to Mr. Penhor and Mr. Lift, despite the growing interest in horror movies in the country, this genre was missing in São Tomean film representations. Also in 2014, Mr. Dodamy Lift founded BNK BEST MOVIES with the purpose of creating movies on and produced in São Tomé and Príncipe by its own people.

The plot of this trilogy is based on a true story: a man, Pinta Cabra,[33] used to steal goats only to resell them to their original owners at a higher price. Mr. Penhor changed the story, adding elements of horror and eeriness while highlighting the beauties of São Tomé and Príncipe.

The terror movie *Viagem sem Volta 1* was directed by Aguinaldo Carvalho and edited by Jerinho Lopes and Ronilson Yong, all from São Tomé and Príncipe. It was produced in 2017 by *Mudaico Filmes* and by BNK BEST MOVIES.

A group of young São Tomeans (four men and three women) go camping. Things go awry when a member of the group goes missing and a strange man wanders the woods starting to slaughter people. The young men and women have one goal now: run as fast they can from the forest of Trindade with Pinta Cabra hunting them down one by one. One member of the group reveals some details about Pinta Cabra's life. Pinta Cabra was a very good man, who lived to serve and help people. He had many farms with many animals and was very rich. Then, one day, a witch arrived and bewitched him. Pinta Cabra became a thief and began stealing animals from other farmers. He would steal goats,

---

[33] Not to be confused with Pinta Cabra, the nickname given to former Prime-Minister of São Tomé and Príncipe, Patrice Émery Trovoada (1962-), who held this position three times: February 14, 2008-June 22, 2008; August 14, 2010-December 12, 2012; and November 25-December 3, 2018. Between September 1, 2001, and February 4, 2002, Trovoada also served as Minister of Foreign Affairs. Currently, Trovoada is Secretary-General of ADI (*Ação Democrática Independente*, Independent Democratic Action), a center, center-right political party founded in 1994 by his father, Miguel Trovoada (1937-), second president of São Tomé and Príncipe (April 3, 1991-September 3, 2001). Patrice Trovoada is known as Pinta Cabra for the alleged corrupt ways with which he conducts his business.

paint them, and then sell them to their original owners. The last goat he stole was a dead goat whose owner was also dead. Pinta Cabra was frightened and began killing people. Eventually the final two members of the group run away. They fight with Pinta Cabra and fire at him. He falls. After a while Pinta Cabra gets up and shows his fiery eyes. This is the end of *Viagem sem Volta 1*.

The terror movie *Viagem sem Volta 2* was directed by Aguinaldo Penhor Carvalho and edited by Dodamy Loureiro. It was produced in 2018 by BNK BEST MOVIES. Five young São Tomeans, three men (Mauro, Benny, and Rafael) and two women (Gina and Laura), are going to the forest Zant and stumble upon a cadaver. The island of São Tomé has a natural park, the *Parque Natural Obô* (Obô Natural Park of São Tomé) whereas the island of Príncipe has the *Parque Natural Obô do Príncipe* (Obô Natural Park of Príncipe). The Zant forest does not exist. When I asked Mr. Penhor why he created such a mysterious forest, he smiled and said that he just wanted to give a touch of horror and weirdness.

The story unravels as the young men and women try to solve the mystery. The main character, Águia, played by Aguinaldo Carvalho, is faced with many obstacles. All of a sudden, a spirit-like young man with his face slightly painted white cuts Benny's head off. The four young campers start running away, fearing for their lives as they begin to meet gruesome fates, with Júlia being the only survivor in the group. Águia eventually encounters Júlia, who tells her that the killer is Pinta Cabra, the devil! The two manage to kill Pinta Cabra near the end of the film. However, The movie ends with an image of a zombie dragging a corpse of a woman. This zombie figure then steps in a body of fresh water. He turns around and shows his fiery, devil-like eyes. He was being possessed by Pinta Cabra.

The terror movie *Viagem sem Volta 3* was directed by Aguinaldo Carvalho and edited by Dodamy Loureiro. It was produced in 2019 by BNK BEST MOVIES with the assistance of the *Centro Cultural Português* of district Mé-Zochi, Trindade, São Tomé, and Mudaico Filmes. *Viagem sem Volta 3* starts with a preview of *Viagem sem Volta 1* and *Viagem sem Volta 2*. In the opening scene, Júlia and Águia are murdered by Pinta Cabra.

The film then cuts to a scene of a bar featuring two young men, Mr. Silva and Mr. Pinky. A radio announcer talks about a major problem and that there is a $2,000 reward for anyone who kills the devil in the forest. Pinky wants the money. He searches the Internet trying to discern who this person is. Success! It is Benzebu (Beelzebub), i.e., Pinta Cabra, also known as Death. Pinky reads that the only way to destroy Benzebu is to make him disappear by destroying a bottle that he has in his possession. Pinky thinks that he will be famous after he kills this man (Pinta Cabra). He calls his friend, Tony, and they make arrangements to hunt down Pinta Cabra, who Pinky believes is just an ordinary guy.

A man, Mr. Júlio, and his wife, Beatriz (Bea), are kissing. Mr. Silva is at the door. Silva tells him that he saw their poster. Silva tells Júlio and Bea that he needs to find his twin brother who has been missing for almost four months. Silva tells them that the Police did not do anything because of the "devil" situation. When Júlio and Bea hear the name of the forest they gasp. Júlio tells Silva that they can go to the forest on the following day. Silva wants to tag along. Júlio tells Silva that he has to pay in advance.

The next day, Silva, Júlio, and Bea enter the forest. Pinky and Tony are also there. Pinta Cabra begins to hunt them down, using magic to force Tony to shoot himself. Pinky calls out Pinta Cabra's name: "Benzebu!" He is calling him names and then says: "Come and get me!" Pinta Cabra begins to strike down the members of the group, despite them getting advice from the spirits of his previous victims, one of which is Águia, whose spirit is trapped on Earth— i.e., in the forest. Águia tells Júlio how to kill Pinta Cabra.

Pinta Cabra chases after Júlio. Júlio fires at Pinta Cabra. Pinta Cabra is on the ground. Júlio retrieves the bottle from Pinta Cabra's pants. Pinta Cabra gets up and eventually kills Júlio by putting a sword through the tree against which Júlio was leaning. Yet, before he died Júlio was able to open the bottle. A black cloud was released. Pinta Cabra falls down, gasping for air. He then dies. The sound of thunder ends the movie.

In 2018, Mudaico Filmes produced the twelve-minute, one-reeler *Jogos Ilegais* (Illegal Games) focusing on illegal activities performed by young São Tomean men and women. Written and directed by Aguinaldo Carvalho and edited by Izequiel Leite, *Jogos Ilegais* features young São Tomean actors Adigar Bull, Aguinaldo Carvalho, José dos Sacramento, Achile Gomes, Izequiel Leite, Dodamy Lift, Perci Neto, Lulu Santos, Luís Silva, Tânia Tavares, and Niki Varela.

The emphasis of this movie is on illegal gambling and betting. A young São Tomean man is accused by the local mob of being a police informer since the local police just raided illegal betting activities at a card-game gathering. Tired of hiding, the young man seeks refuge in drinking. Drunk at a local bar he is counseled by his old friend, now a born-again Christian who encourages him to change his life. The police eventually apprehend the illegal gamblers and the young snitch changes his life. He went to church, became a born-again Christian, went to school, and earned a degree. His advice to the audience is to quit gambling and doing drugs, money laundering, and other criminal activities. His final words are: "O seu futuro depende de si."[34]

---

[34] "Filme Jogos Ilegais – São Tomé e Príncipe – África Curta metragem." <https://youtu.be/N1HPl7VrRG4>. "Your future is in your hands." [translated by the author].

In 2020, Mudaico Filmes released *A Luta pela Sobrevivência* (The Struggle for Survival), a horror movie featuring Aguinaldo Carvalho, Luís Sila, Jair Rita, Izequiel Stock, and Jamila Soares. [35] Directed and written by Aguinaldo Carvalho, *A Luta pela Sobrevivência* continues along the lines of the *Viagem sem Volta 1, 2*, and *3* trilogy whereby the main characters have to struggle for their survival in the forest. A group of young men and women assault a young man, played by Heitor Mendim. Once recovered, the victim plots his relentless revenge against his assailants since, as he asserts, "[…] infelizmente não sei perdoar."[36]

São Tomé and Príncipe: Final Remarks

> Desde os documentários coloniais até à contemporaneidade, a história do cinema e do audiovisual em São Tomé e Príncipe é feita de fragmentos e lacunas, mas também de memórias, e das novas experiências que pretendem revitalizar a área da imagem em movimento. (Falconi and Karkowska 2017, 190)[37]

As Alessandra Meleiro stated, filmmaking in Lusophone Africa portrays "the struggle for socio-cultural change involved" in "decolonizing "of film-making itself — in all its modes of production, distribution, and screening" (Meleiro 2011, 138). The key word here is "decolonizing" the art of filmmaking since, even though there are still Westerners involved in producing documentaries and films on African issues, Westerners and Africans alike are now contributing to the creation of a film industry that is truly local, addressing local issues and needs.

As for São Tomé and Príncipe, the seven documentaries mentioned above and the four community-awareness, big-screen projects *O Fogo do Apagar a Vida* (The Fire Extinguishing Life, 2002), produced by Januário Afonso that focuses on HIV-AIDS, *Vosso Amor, o Meu Sorriso* (Your Love, My Smile, 2007), directed by Januário Afonso on domestic violence, *Em Pequenos Mundos* (In Small Worlds, 2013), produced by Caló Costa following the lives of young boys and girls wandering the streets of São Tomé and Príncipe, and *O Avesso da Vida* (The Opposite of Life, 2014), produced by Januário Afonso and Kalú Mendes on

---

[35] "Bastidores do Filme, A Luta pela Sobrevivência, 2020." <https://youtu.be/vlZ509xq88I>.
[36] <https://www.facebook.com/Mudaico-Filmes-877940065714960/>. "[…] unfortunately I do not know how to forgive." [translated by the author].
[37] "From the colonial documentaries to the present-day, the history of cinema and audiovisual in São Tomé and Príncipe is made of fragments and lacunae, but also of memories, and of new experiences that aim at revitalizing the area of the image in movement." [translated by the author].

the life of the elderly in São Tomé and Príncipe, are in a sense a necessary preamble to the birth of a new film genre in São Tomé and Príncipe.

Indeed, the changes proposed by Mudaico Filmes are bold; yet, they address a need, the need of young and not-so-young São Tomeans who enjoy exploring the eerie, the macabre, and the unknown, surrounded by the majestic nature of their country, where the supernatural aids the eternal struggle of good vs. evil.

Works Cited

Almada, André Álvares Gonçalves de. *Relação e Descrição da Guiné, na Qual se Trata de Várias Nações de Negros Que a Povoam, dos Seus Costumes, Leis, Ritos, Cerimonias, Trajos, da Qualidade dos Portos e do Comércio Que neles Se Faz. Escreveu o Capitão André Gonçalves de Almada*; André Álvares Gonçalves de Almada. *Tratado Breve dos Rios da Guiné do Cabo-Verde*. 1594. Ed. António Luís Ferronha. Lisbon: Comissão Nacional para as Comemorações dos Descobrimentos Portugueses, 1994.

___. *Tratado Breve dos Rios da Guiné do Cabo-Verde*. 1594. Ed. António Luís Ferronha. Lisbon: Comissão Nacional para as Comemorações dos Descobrimentos Portugueses, 1994.

Amado, Leopoldo. "A Literatura Colonial Guineense." *Revista ICALP* 20-21 (Julho – Outubro, 1990): 160-178.

Andrade-Watkins, Claire. "Portuguese African Cinema: Historical and Contemporary Perspectives—1969-1993." *Research in African Literatures* (1995): 134-150.

Arenas, Fernando. *Lusophone Africa: Beyond Independence*. Minneapolis: University of Minnesota Press, 2011.

Brunel, Raphael. "Filipa César", in *Frieze*. March 30 2013. frieze.com/article/filipa-cesar.

Burness, Donald. "The Literature of Cape Verde, São Tomé and Príncipe." *Zeitschrift für Kulturaustausch* 29 (1979): 183-188.

Cardina, Miguel. "Luta ca caba inda: from archive to fragment." *Afroscreen* 2019.

César, Filipa. "A Grin Without Marker." *L'Internatiopnale* 2016. Online.

Chaves, Marina Oliveira Félix de Mello, and Bruna Suelen Rocha Miranda. "As produções cinematográficas dos Países Africanos de Língua Oficial Portuguesa." Leitura: *Teoria & Prática* 35. 70 (2017): 33-49.

Choudhury, Beatrice. "The Archaeology of Film: Close-Up on Filipa César's "Spell Reel." Mubi.com October 21, 2017. https://mubi.com/notebook/posts/the-archaeology-of-film-close-up-on-filipa-cesar-s-spell-reel.

CPS. Filipa César." *Manifesta 8*. 09/10/10-09/01/11. http://arpa.carm.es/manifesta/manifesta8.artist?nombre=Filipa-C%E9sar&codigo=66.

Damas, Léon Gontran. *Pigments*. Paris: G.L.M., 1937.

Falconi, Jessica, and Kamila Krakowska. "Panorama do Cinema do Audiovisual em São Tomé e Príncipe." *Mulemba* 9. 17 (jul/dez 2017): 177-193.

Federação Portuguesa de Cineclubes. https://www.fpcc.pt/lojaneves/.

"Filipa César: 'Luta ca caba inda'." *Making Art Happen.* October 16, 2012. https://makingarthappen.com/2012/10/16/filipa-cesar-luta-ca-caba-inda/.

Ferreira, Carolin Overhoff. "Ambivalent Transnationality: Luso-African Co-Productions after Independence (1988-2010)." *Journal of Cinemas* 3 2 (2011): 221-245.

___. "Decolonizing the Mind? The Representation of the African Colonial War in Portuguese Cinema." *Studies in European Cinema* 2.3 (2005): 227-239.

___. "Entre a Transgressão e a Afirmação da 'Lei do Pai': Algumas Protagonistas do Cinema Português nos Anos Noventa," in *Mulheres Más: Percepção e Representações da Mulher Transgressora no Mundo Luso-Hispânico.* Eds. Ana Maria da Costa Toscano, and Shelly Godsland. vol. 1. Porto: Universidade Fernando Pessoa, 2004. 1: 105-120.

Ferreira, Manuel. *Literatura africana dos países de expressão portuguesa.* vol. 1. Biblioteca Breve/Volume 6. Lisbon: Instituto de Cultura Portuguesa, 1977.

"Filipa César." *MUBI.* https://mubi.com/cast/filipa-cesar.

Glessing, Jill. "Filipa César: Spell Reel." C Magazine. 139 (Fall 2018). https://cmagazine.com/issues/139/filipa-csar-spell-reel.

Hamilton, Russell G. *Literatura Africana. Literatura Necessária.* 2. *Moçambique, Cabo Verde, Guiné-Bissau, São Tomé e Príncipe.* Lisbon: Edições 70, 1984.

ICA. "As memórias de São Tomé e Príncipe começam hoje a ser recordadas." *Instituto do Cinema e do Audiovisual* February 15 2017. https://www.ica-ip.pt/pt/noticias/as-memorias-de-sao-tome-e-principe-comecam-hoje-a-ser-recordadas/.

Kenigsberg, Ben. "Review: 'Spell Reel' Shows a Revolution Filmed, on the Leader's Orders." *The New York Times* June 27, 2017. https://www.nytimes.com/2017/06/27/movies/spell-reel-review-guinea-bissau.html

Laranjeira, Pires. "Introdução," in *Negritude Africana de Língua Portuguesa. Textos de Apoio (1947-1963).* Ed. Pires Laranjeria. Braga: Angelus Novus, 2000. vii-xxi.

Leite, Ana Mafalda, Jessica Falconi Kamila Krakowska, Sheila Kahn, and Carmen Tindó Secco, eds. *Voices, Languages, Discourses. Interpreting the Present and the Memory of Nation in Cape Verde, Guinea-Bissau, and São Tomé and Príncipe.* Oxford: Peter Lang, 2020.

Levi, Joseph Abraham. "The Many Identity Markers of Luso-Americas: Linguistic and Psychological Identities among First-, Second-, and Third-Generation Portuguese-Americans." *International Journal of Arts and Social Science* 3 3 (May-June 2020): 277-301.

___. "Intérpretes, escravos e almas necessitadas. Os africanos no espaço luso-atlântico dos primórdios," in *Senhores e Escravos nas Sociedades Ibero-Atlânticas.* Eds. Maria do Rosário Pimentel, and Maria do Rosário Monteiro. Lisbon: CHAM, Centro de Umanidades, Faculdade de Ciências Sociais e Humanas da Universidade NOVA de Lisboa, Universidade dos Açores, 2019 [2020]. 209-226.

___. "São Tomé e Príncipe: Um Laboratório Atlântico: Diásporas e Dinâmicas Literárias," in *Livro de Actas: Colóquio Internacional São Tomé e Príncipe numa perspectiva interdisciplinar, diacrónica e sincrónica.* Eds. Ana Cristina Roque, Gerhard Seibert, and Vítor Rosado Marques. Lisbon: Instituto

Universitário de Lisboa (ISCTE-IUL), Centro de Estudos Africanos (CEA-IUL), Instituto de Investigação Científica Tropical (IICT), 2012. 349-368.

___. "Cabo Verde e São Tomé: Divergências e semelhanças literárias." *Mentalities/Mentalités* 18.2 (2004): 15-25.

Lopes, Manuel. "Prefácio," in *Across the Atlantic: An Anthology of Cape Verdean Literature*. Ed. Maria M. Ellen. North Dartmouth, MA: Center for the Portuguese Speaking World, 1988. vi-x.

"M. Cardoso Furtado." CINEPT – CINEMA PORTUGUÊS. http://www.cinept. ubi.pt/pt/pessoa/2143688896/M.+Cardoso+Furtado.

Margarido, Manuela. "Le poids des valeurs portugais dans la poésie de Francisco José Tenreiro," in *Les littératures africaines d'expression portugaise: A la recherche de l'identité individuelle et nationale*. Paris: Fundação Calouste Gulbenkian, 1985. 429-436.

Martins, Celso. "Correspondências abertas." *Expresso*. June 15, 2019. https:// expresso.pt/cultura/2019-06-15-Correspondencias-abertas.

McNeil, Gabby. "Turning a Blind Eyes to Slavery: the Cadbury Company." Chocolate Class. Multimedia Essays on Chocolate, Culture, and the Politics of Food. November 3, 2016. https://chocolateclass.wordpress.com/2016/03/ 11/turning-a-blind-eye-to-slavery-the-cadbury-company/.

Meleiro, Alessandra. "Luso-African Cinema: Nation and Cinema." *Journal of African Cinema* 3 2 (2011): 135-138.

"Memórias de São Tomé e Príncipe – São Tomé FESTFILM '17." *Téla Nón* February 13 2017. https://www.telanon.info/cultura/2017/02/13/23773/ memorias-de-sao-tome-e-principe-sao-tome-festfilm17/.

"MoMa Presents: Filipa César's Spell Reel." (2017) Moma.org. https://www. moma.org/calendar/film/3846.

Piçarra, Maria do Carmo. "Cinema Império: a projeção colonial do Estado Novo português nos filmes das exposições entre guerras mundiais." *Outros Tempos* 13. 22 (2016): 126-151.

"Portuguese Artist Filipa César Presents "The Struggle is not Over Yet" at Jeu de Paume." *Art Daily* October 30 2012. https://artdaily.cc/news/58480/ Portuguese-artist-Filipa-C-sar-presents--The-struggle-is-Not-Over-Yet--at-Jeu-de-Paume#.XiXT28hKiM8.

Rodrigues, João Carlos. *O Negro Brasileiro e o Cinema*. Rio de Janeiro: Pallas, 2001.

Roof, María. "African and Latin American Cinemas: Contexts and Contacts," in Françoise Pfaff, ed. *Focus on African Filmes*. Bloomington: Indiana University Press, 2004. 241-270.

Rosenbaum, Jonathan. "Personal Effects: The Guarded Intimacy of Sans Soleil." *Criterion*, June 25, 2007. https://www.criterion.com/current/posts/484-personal-effects-the-guarded-intimacy-of-sans-soleil.

Rothwell, Phillip. "Inventing a Lusotropical Father, or, The Neurotic Legacy in Germano Almeida's *O Testamento do Senhor Napumoceno*." *Research in African Literatures* 38.1 (Spring 2007): 95-105.

Rothwell, Phillip, and Ana Maria Martinho. "Introduction. Four Decades of Independence: The Multiple Cultures of Portuguese-Speaking Africa." *Journal of Lusophone Studies* 1. 1 (Spring 2016): 1-6.

Samy, Domingas Barbosa Mendes. *A Escola. Contos*. Bissau: Editora Escolar, 1993.

"Santomense Ângelo no único festival de cinema celebrado em simultâneo na Europa e na África." *Téla Nón* March 19, 2018. https://www.telanon.info/cultura/2018/03/19/26594/santomense-angelo-torres-no-unico-festival-de-cinema-celebrado-em-simultaneo-na-europa-e-na-africa/.

"Seis Filmes da África Lusófona Nomeados para Prémio António Loja Neves." *Correio da Manhã* April 23 2019. https://www.correiodamanhacanada.com/seis-filmes-da-africa-lusofona-nomeados-para-premio-antonio-loja-neves/.

Spell Reel: Cinept – Cinema Português. 2017. http://www.cinept.ubi.pt/pt/filme/10320/Spell+Reel.

Spell Reel: Filipa César. "Cinéma du réel. 42e festival international du film documentaire. 13-22 mars 2020." *Cinéma du réel*. http://www.cinemadureel.org/film/spell-reel-2/?lang=en.

Spell Reel: NWFILM.ORG. nwfilm.org/films/spell-reel.

Ukadike, N. Frank. "The Hyena's Last Laugh. A Conversation with Djibril Diop Mambety." *Transition* 78.8 2 (1999): 136-153.

Chapter 5

On Camera, In Motion: Staging São Tomé e Príncipe in Contemporary Film

Daniel F. Silva
Middlebury College

Abstract

Since independence in 1975, genres of São Toméan cultural production that have garnered the most critical attention and widespread consumption have been poetry and music. The São Toméan literary canon, though notably dominated by black women poets such as Alda Espírito Santo, Olinda Beja, and Conceição Lima, has been largely consumed and defined in the former colonial metropolis by academics and literary critics. Meanwhile, different genres constituting the landscape of popular music, includingÚssua, Socopé, and Kizomba, have become increasingly consumed internationally in various Lusophone spaces and retracing Portuguese imperial cartographies, as well as in global northern Anglophone markets under the problematic category of world music. Little attention, however, has been paid to film in São Tomé e Príncipe, though there has been a long and fraught history of colonial and postcolonial film production that has revolved around particular images of São Toméan space and bodies, through which colonial othering has met postcolonial signification of national singularity. This essay will offer a brief genealogy of colonial and postcolonial film until 2000, before interrogating how subsequent generations of filmmakers, harnessing different modes of dissemination and consumption, have radically revised the imagery of exoticism and essentialization that characterized colonial film and much of postcolonial production circuited to metropolitan consumption.

The aesthetic urgency of rendering national identity and signifying national space following empire and its remaining structural legacies can be found in literary, musical, and visual production. Through continued colonial means of cultural consumption and international circulation dominated by global northern recording companies, publishing houses, film studios/production companies, and audiences, such production has often been rerouted into trends of consumptive exoticization. Against the dangers of postcolonial exoticization and abjection that have rendered African postcoloniality through stereotyped images of modernity's radical other and capitalism's peripheral locale par excellence – political instability, economic stagnation, inefficient exploitation of land, disease, and invalid knowledge – contemporary filmmakers like Valeri André Menezes, Juelce Beija Flor, Kátia Aragão, and Aguinaldo Carvalho have looked to construct stories and signify bodies in ways that challenge globally hegemonic discourses concerning Africa. In this sense, in striving to create contemporary visual aesthetics that render São Toméan space and quotidian life beyond the globally hyper-consumed images of African societies, such filmmakers offer productions that move away from colonial tropes while also expanding the limits and prerogatives of postcolonial anti-hegemonic film aesthetics such as those of the Third Cinema movement.

Keywords: São Tomé and Príncipe, Third Cinema, nationalism, postcolonialism

* * *

Since independence in 1975, genres of São Toméan cultural production that have garnered the most critical attention and widespread consumption have been poetry and music. The São Toméan literary canon, though notably dominated by black women poets such as Alda Espírito Santo, Olinda Beja, and Conceição Lima, has been largely consumed and defined in the former colonial metropolis by academics and literary critics. Meanwhile, different genres constituting the landscape of popular music, including Ússua, Socopé, and Kizomba, have become increasingly consumed internationally in various Lusophone spaces and retracing Portuguese imperial cartographies, as well as in Global Northern Anglophone markets under the problematic category of world music. Little attention, however, has been paid to film in São Tomé e Príncipe. This is due in some measure to a dearth of film production in the archipelago's colonial and postcolonial history, though there is a complex history to be told on this lack as well as on the productions that have circulated, particularly those most recently from young filmmakers in light of missing institutions and traditions of national cinema.

São Tomé e Príncipe did appear, and was configured as colonial space, in some Portuguese colonial visual media, especially in works staging the large cocoa plantations during the twentieth century. These would become objects of international investigations in the early 1900s concerned with the use of slave labor after denunciations by English travelers and officials, culminating in a series of reports such as those of Joseph Burtt and William A. Cadbury, of 1907 and 1910. The latter writer was part of the Cadbury multinational confectionary family known for its chocolate products, and thus conceivably had a vested interest in denouncing labor practices from an imperial competitor in São Tomé e Príncipe, at the time the largest producer of cocoa in the world. Conflicts of interest aside with regards to Cadbury's report, the Portuguese response to the allegations did little to alibi Portuguese plantation owners and colonial authorities. Rather, the response to Burtt's report, "Portugal e o regime do trabalho indígena nas suas colónias," (Curto, 1959, 62) published in 1910, defended Portuguese labor practices as a civilizing tool by which *índigenas* would become *assimilados*, and thus gain institutional privilege, or an illusion thereof.

It was this inter-imperial conflict and political ordeal that drove the earliest cinematic representations of colonial São Tomé e Príncipe. The Portuguese report essentially followed up on *A cultura do Cacau [Cacao Culture]* (1909), directed by Ernesto de Albuquerque, the first motion picture production on São Tomé e Príncipe financed by the state, a constitutional monarchy until 1910. The documentary, of which only one minute has survived, was produced to depict a benevolent colonial society in which laborers, often captured and imported from Angola, were compensated and treated with dignity by their employers. In this same propagandistic logic, the following year saw the release of a documentary titled, *O Cacau Escravo e Trabalho Indígena em S. Tomé [Slave Cacao and Indigenous Labor in São Tomé]*, by Cardoso Furtado, at the Geographical Society of Lisbon. Early images of São Tomé e Príncipe, still or moving, thus served to portray a Portuguese civilizing mission carried out via labor while also staging empire as integral to Portugueseness. As Fernando Arenas underscores, "Ultimately, Portuguese colonial cinema was another important ideological vehicle through which to assert Portuguese national identity as tied to empire as well as to construct Portuguese settler identity" (Arenas 2011, 108).

In the decades of the mid-twentieth century, São Tomé e Príncipe and the subalternized bodies inhabiting it would become ideologically inserted into a multi-continental and multiracial narrativization of Portuguese national identity promulgated by António Oliveira Salazar, dictator of the fascist Estado Novo [New State] regime from 1933-1968. Visual footage of Portugal's African colonies, therefore, also became a vehicle to stage multiracial and multicontinental Portugal while still foregrounding an imperial system of representation schematizing geo-cultural and corporal difference in conjunction with racialized and gendered orders of power. Such footage included postcards, stamps, journalistic photography, and film produced through the Estado Novo's Secretariado Nacional de Informação, Cultura Popular, e Turismo [National Secretariat of Information, Popular Culture, and Tourism] (SNI).

Different state entities under and even prior to the Estado Novo created their own production companies. These included the Serviços Cinematográficos do

Exército [Cinematic Services of Military] and Missão Cinegráfica às Colónias de África [Cinematographic Mission to the Colonies of Africa], created in 1937 by then Minister of the Colonies, Francisco Vieira Machado. The former produced, via filmmaker Augusto Seara, spans Guinea-Bissau and São Tomé e Príncipe – *Por Terras de Ébano* [*Through Ebony Lands*] of 1929. The same company also produced the documentary, *São Tomé Agrícola e Industrial* [*Agricultural and Industrial São Tomé*], in the same year. In both, São Tomé e Príncipe appears as part of Portuguese imperial cartography and an object of imperial knowledge through the film's ethnographic objectives of classifying bodies and spaces into an imperial system of representation. A similar theme and mission informed other documentaries that included footage of San Toméan locales and inhabitants, including Fernandes Thomaz's *A Colónia de Moçambique* [*The Colony of Mozambique*] (1931), despite its title, via yet another company, the Brigada Cinematográfica Portuguesa [Portuguese Cinematographic Brigade]. Filmmakers António Antunes Mata and José César de Sá also produced a series of films on the colonies with a similar gaze, including *De Lisboa a São Tomé* [*From Lisbon to São Tomé*] (1933).

The history of colonial film production on São Tomé e Príncipe reveals many continuities of economic power gained by particular Portuguese families and corporations in former colonies, and how these exercise global power today. For instance, the 1929 documentary and earliest recorded feature-length production on São Tomé e Príncipe, *Uma Visita às Propriedades da Sociedade Agrícola Valle Flor* [*A Visit to the Properties of the Valle Flor Agricultural Society*], funded by the Portuguese Cinematographic Brigade, sought to stage (the arguably sanitized) labor practices and everyday operations of one particular cacao plantation/estate as an example of the Portuguese civilizing mission in Africa. The owner of the plantation, José Constantino Dias was given the royal title of Marquis of Valle Flor in 1907 after having the title of Viscount of Valle Flor by royal in 1890. The Sociedade Agrícola Valle Flor operates today in São Tomé e Príncipe and is headquartered in Lisbon, as a joint-stock corporation, sold by the family in 2009. The Valle Flor family continues to possess numerous holdings in different economic sectors in the Lusophone world, and operates the Instituto Marquês Valle Flor, today an NGO working on public health and development issues in Africa and Latin America ("Who We Are"). Originally founded by Dias's wife, Dona Maria do Carmo Dias Constantino Ferreira Pinto, in 1951, the institute served as a eugenic research institute to produce "trabalhos científicos sobre colonização em geral, condições de vida nas províncias ultramarinas portuguesas, especialmente na ilha de S. Tomé, nos seus aspectos social, moral, sanitário e económico, e possibilidades de melhoria dessas condições sobre flora e fauna das mesmas províncias" ["scientific works concerning colonization in general, living conditions in the Portuguese overseas provinces, especially in São Tomé, in its social, moral, sanitary, and economic facets, in addition to the chances of improving said conditions over the flora and fauna in these provinces" Instituto Marquês de Valle Flôr 1951). These histories are inextricably linked to contemporary local and global structures of postcolonial inequity that reverberate in the landscape of cultural production, especially in the realm of film whereby production is often contingent upon funding from corporations and foundations that select which projects are to be supported.

Following the rise of the Estado Novo, the aforementioned Cinematographic Mission to the Colonies of Africa (MCCA) produced an extensive collection of films on the imperial expansiveness of Portuguese nationhood. As Patrícia Ferraz de Matos explains, the MCCA's productions straddled reproducing the exoticized images and texts of African otherness and staging Portuguese civilizational development in African colonies (156-57). As such, in their films "buscava-se um retrato da selva, dos animais, dos 'batuques,' mas também de uma África 'civilizada,' com cidades grandes em desenvolvimento" (Matos 2006, 157), as indicated by titles such as *Gentes que Nós Civilizamos* [*Peoples We Have Civilized*] (1944) and *As Ilhas Crioulas de Cabo Verde* [*The Creole Islands of Cabo Verde*] (1945).

São Tomé e Princípe and its inhabitants were also always implicitly invoked through the articulation and cartography of a multicontinental Portugal. In one of the more circulated productions staging Portuguese imperial discourses, one that summoned collective input from the Portuguese public via an entry contest for the film's plot, *Feitiço do Império* [*The Spell of the Empire*] (1940), the protagonist, Luís Morais, a young Portuguese-American man from Boston, is convinced by his wealthy father to travel through Portugal's African colonies in order to dissuade him from marrying his American fiancée. The plot fundamentally pits two imperial/settler colonial nation-building projects and their respective narratives against one another. Directed by António Lopes Ribeiro, the film follows Luís as he grows up in Boston and is fascinated by American society, with his love for his fiancée, Fay Gordon, functioning as a stand-in for his infatuation with US empire. By traveling to Lisbon (imperial metropolis) and the Portuguese colonies, he comes to favor the Estado Novo's supposed model of empire, based on benevolent multiculturalism and multi-continentality. The film, despite focusing on settler society in Angola, implicitly integrates Portugal's other colonies in its evocation of the *além-mar* or *ultra-mar* (overseas Portugal). Notwithstanding the Estado Novo's claims of a multicultural horizontal society built by empire rather than an assimilationist one, the film stages colonial orders of bodies, power, and knowledge in myriad ways – a racial division of labor, Portuguese colonists teaching native children Portuguese as the valid language, and settler cultural practices such as hunting. As Patrícia Vieira points out in her critical analysis of the film, Luís ultimately rejects American values and is "converted" to imperial Portugueseness (Viera 2010, 135). Films such as this one became part of a broader and sustained ideological and pedagogical apparatus deployed by the Estado Novo to incentivize working-class and rural Portuguese citizens to migrate to the colonies (Castello 2007) rather than to the Americas and other European countries.

Some of the footage used by Lopes Ribeiro, especially of landscapes, came from his documentary of the year prior, *Viagem do Chefe de Estado às Colónias de Angola e São Tomé e Príncipe* [*The Chief of State's Voyage to the Colonies of Angola and São Tomé e Príncipe*] (1939), following Óscar Carmona's visit, from his disembark to his travels through the respective colonies`. The success of this visit and subsequent film led to a sequel the following year after Carmona's second visit. *A Segunda Viagem Triunfal* [*The Second Triumphant Voyage*] made deeper historical connections between the staged grandeur of Portuguese colonial settlement and the long historicization of Portuguese empire, particularly through a scene of a street parade through colonial Maputo (then Lourenço Marques) containing floats depicting the voyages of Vasco da Gama, the conquest of Mozambique, and visual maps of a multicontinental Portugal.

In the late 1950s and early 1960s, up until the armed anti-colonial struggle that marked the latter decade, the aesthetics of Portuguese colonial film intensified the Estado Novo's public embrace of Lusotropicalist narratives of Portuguese overseas provinces (as they were renamed in official rhetoric) that were multiracial societies. This implied a revised rhetoric of an expansive nation-state into which empire was dovetailed with Brazilian anthropologist Gilberto Freyre's theory of Lusotropicalism. Freyre's historicizing project drew on lines of thought from earlier Portuguese and Brazilian intellectuals, and posited Portuguese imperial endeavor as guided less by economic gain than by an inherent and collective drive toward forming a multiracial community. Freyre, like intellectuals before him, built this argument on a foundational narrative of a Portuguese hybrid ethos stemming from Roman, Visigothic, and Arab occupation. Documentaries such as *Comunidade Luso-Brasileira* [*Portuguese-Brazilian Community*] of 1958, *Terra Mãe* [*Motherland*] of 1960, *Nossos Irmãos, os Africans* [*Our Brethren, the Africans*] of 1963, and *Catembe* of 1965 all sought to stage a supposedly horizontal (un)colonial social environment in which the structural and physical violence of other European national imperial projects was absent.

From Colonial Film to Postcolonial National Cinema

Throughout the early and mid-twentieth century, Portuguese colonial cinema, though sparse in volume when compared to other European powers, participated in the visual culture of empires of the time, with presence in colonial exhibits and screenings in world's fairs and international expositions. In comparison with Angola, Cabo Verde, and Mozambique (Portugal's other African colonies), São Tomé e Príncipe and Guinea-Bissau did not figure as prominently in Portuguese colonial cinema. Relatedly, Portuguese colonial authorities did not create an institutional infrastructure for cinematic production or consumption in São Tomé e Príncipe comparable to those of other colonies, especially Angola and Mozambique, where the Portuguese state invested more resources and established settler communities in the twentieth century (Castelo 2007,10). Moreover, in comparison with the greater impetus on film production placed by other European colonial powers in Africa, the vestiges of colonial cinema were scarce in Lusophone Africa at the moment of independence (1975, with the exception of Guinea-Bissau which declared independence in 1973), according to Clyde Taylor (1983, 30). As Claire Andrade-Watkins highlights, the rise of film in Lusophone Africa was propelled by liberation movements with "external support from the international community for the revolutionary war efforts" (Andrade-Watkins 1995, 136) and continued after independence.

The development of anti-colonial and then post-independence national cinemas was thus tied to armed struggles for independence and then postcolonial proxy wars/civil wars, with international financial assistance offered to ruling parties – PAIGC (African Party for the Independence of Guinea-Bissau and Cabo Verde), FRELIMO (Liberation Front of Mozambique), and MPLA (People's Movement for the Liberation of Angola). São Tomé e Príncipe's leading liberation group then post-independence ruling party, MLSTP (Movement for the Liberation of São Tomé e Príncipe) was the only triumphant movement of Lusophone Africa not to be engaged in armed struggle for independence. As the main liberation movement of São Tomé e Príncipe, its leaders and operations were based mainly in Gabon until the post-revolutionary government succeeding the Estado Novo in Portugal in 1974 transferred power to the MLSTP in 1975. Because power in São Tomé was transferred without a sustained armed struggle, and without post-independence military conflict, film did not develop in the archipelago as it did in other Lusophone African postcolonial nations as a vehicle through which to articulate war efforts to the masses and garner popular support while fomenting national consciousness. Cabo Verde, though integrated with Guinea-Bissau into one party, did not become a war front, but had begun developing an interest in cinematic production and consumption decades prior to the armed struggles of the 1960s and 70s, led largely by intellectuals who had studied in Lisbon and through growing Pan-African epistemologies and cultural production.

The growth of liberation cinema as part of anti-colonial struggle can be placed in the same global archive of cultural engagement against forces of empire as the Third Cinema movement articulated by Argentinean filmmakers Fernando Solanas and Octavio Gettino's manifesto, "Towards a Third Cinema." After independence, this engagement was at the heart of the nation-building projects envisioned by Lusophone African postcolonial ruling parties, all of which took up strong ideological positions against global capitalism and its intersections with the long-durée history of Western imperialism. As opposed to the case of San Toméan cinema, filmmaking played a crucial role in this form of cultural engagement in postcolonial Lusophone Africa, with Mozambique and Angola being the most active cases. Both of these national cinemas developed not only through possessing some infrastructure left from colonial cinema (i.e. production houses and theaters), but also through key national figures such as Ruy Guerra of Mozambique and Mário Pinto de Andrade of Angola. Guerra, a key contributor to the Cinema Novo movement in Brazil, helped establish the Institute of Cinema in his native Mozambique. Both Angolan and Mozambican cinema also benefitted from greater foreign investment from Cuba, China, and the Soviet Union, while also collaborating with renowned filmmakers such as Jean Rouch, Jean-Luc Godard, Sarah Maldoror, and Jean-René Debrix. Guinea-Bissau's government would go on to fund the development of national cinema, beginning in the 1980s, with or without financial support from international entities, leading to the rise to fame of Flora Gomes following his films *Mortu Nega* [*Death Denied*] (1988) and *Udju Azul di Yonta* [*The Blue Eyes of Yonta*] (1992).

Film production in São Tomé e Príncipe was born through less sustained efforts in comparison to Lusophone African counterparts. Renato Lima, who worked in post-independence São Tomé e Príncipe's Ministry of Information, credits famed São Toméan poet Alda Espírito Santo with propelling the development and use of the moving image among politicians. As a result, the government funded the purchase of a 16mm camera so that the Department of Photography and Cinema of the Ministry of Information could film brief documentaries or journalistic exposés on the political endeavors of MLSTP officials, religious festivals, and other ceremonies (Falconi & Krakowska 2017, 181). The Ministry of Information would then project the films to rural audiences across the islands via mobile cinema, as a vehicle of nation-building. The MLSTP also sent three of its young film operators to Mozambique in the early 1980s to learn production techniques from the aforementioned Mozambican Institute of Cinema. During this period, the Ministry of Information also established a relationship with the Institute whereby the former would send its raw footage to the latter where it would be edited and prepared for dissemination.

The use of mobile cinema would dwindle in the mid and late 1980s with the MLSTP's embrace of television as a vehicle for mass communication and cultural consumption. Falconi and Krakowska (2017) argue that the founding of TVS (São Toméan Public Television) in 1992, with the financial support of Portugal's state-owned network, RTP, marked the end of an era in São Toméan film and the dawning of a new period. The late 1980s up to the present have seen the rise of international co-productions, with São Toméan filmmakers finding funding through the Community of Portuguese-Speaking Countries (CPLP), as well as the growth of for-television film production, as television and access to it have grown steadily. This trend, running parallel to governmental distancing from Marxist-Leninist economic policies, has been accompanied by greater interest from filmmakers and production houses in catering to global audiences and situating their works within dominant global aesthetics of visual culture. This has, of course, implied a straddling between western/global northern aesthetic expectations and challenging western systems of representation.

This period of international co-productions saw the making and release of São Tomé e Príncipe's first feature-length film, *Little Fruit: At the Equator Everything is Possible* (1998), an Austrian, German, and São Toméan co-production. The film, by Herbert Brödl, set and filmed entirely in São Tomé e Príncipe, blends documentary, comedy, fantasy, and road movie genres. The plot follows a young São Toméan man who, as a result of his mother's distant call as she dies, has his life upended by a gigantic breadfruit – the magical materialization of his mother's call – that falls at his door. As a result, he must find ingenious ways of transporting the enormous fruit as he treks to find his mother, drawing an array of reactions and obstacles from onlookers and interveners. His journey intertwines legacies of the colonial past, present socioeconomic structures, and interrogation into São Toméan cultural life, albeit while arguably satisfying global northern consumptive desires for cultural packagings of an exotic Africa and/or of an aesthetic of underdevelopment. Although considered a São Toméan film with regards to cast, location, and plot, the signifying processes surrounding the film's production were dominated by a largely European production team and staff, and for a largely European audience, premiering at the Hof International Film Festival and Lübeck Nordic Film Days.

The production of *Little Fruit* nonetheless included a significant number of São Toméan film crew members that would later work on other important pieces of recent national film history. The same is also true of other large co-productions, such as the 2010 São Toméan-Canadian documentary, *Extra Bitter: The Legacy of the Chocolate Islands*, by Derek Vertongen. Drawing on an interview with one such crew member, Januário Afonso, today a filmmaker of note in his own right, Falconi and Krakowska underscore the dependence on foreign co-productions felt by contemporary filmmakers: "em São Tomé há falta de equipamento e este é trazido pela equipe estrangeira e levado de volta quando as filmagens acabam" ["in São Tomé, there is a lack of equipment, which is usually brought over by foreign crews and returned when shooting concludes" (Falconi and Krakowska 2017, 183). Much São Toméan film production has thus depended on, in addition to co-production, financial assistance from governmental and non-governmental agencies such as the aforementioned CPLP, the Red Cross, the international charity Santa Casa da Misericórdia, the French embassy in São Tomé, and corporations from various sectors including local tourist hotels. Such productions were strategically financed as the proposed film content fit the financier's ends. This is the case with the 48-minute documentary, *A Ilha do Príncipe: O Éden Esquecido do Atlântico* [*The Island of Príncipe: The Forgotten Eden of the Atlantic*] (2014), by Portuguese filmmaker João Teles de Vasconcelos, produced through the NGO Aidnature (co-founded by Vasconcelos), and financed by two luxury hotels on the island of Príncipe – Bom Bom Island Resort and Omali Lodge Resort.

Through its financiers, the film contributes to long-standing (post)colonial exoticist imagery through which São Tomé e Príncipe is consumed by its implied global audiences – a space, as the title indicates, untouched by the forces of modernity, advertised especially to environmental tourists. Even more revealing of this point, the film's production company, Aidnature, is listed and based as an academic center focused on environmental education at the University of Lisbon, and described as producers of knowledge:

Chegam ao destino como exploradores. Nas mochilas, levam os instrumentos de trabalho:

a curiosidade, o entusiasmo e a vontade de dar a conhecer. Descobrem espécies, cores, cheiros, de lugares que fazem questão de observar e investigar, ao pormenor. Desvendam paisagens, caminhos, cantos e recantos que transmitem em imagens apelativas. [...]

Esta é a Aidnature. Uma organização que dá a conhecer a natureza dos países de língua portuguesa, dedicando-se, em exclusivo, à "educação ambiental através da produção e divulgação de conteúdos média altamente apelativos."

[They arrive at their destination like explorers. In their backpacks, they take their tools: curiosity, enthusiasm, and the desire to unearth and teach. They discover species, colors, smells, of locales they observe and research, in detail. They unveil landscapes, trails, and nooks that they transmit through appealing images. (...)

This is Aidnature. An organization that unearths and educates on the natural landscape of Portuguese-speaking countries, dedicated exclusively to "environmental education via the production and dissemination of highly appealing media content."] ("Aidnature")

The organization's description reads like an early modern imperial treatise in defense of western scientific expansion. In Aidnature's work, São Tomé e Príncipe is thus an object of study and inscription within the greater goal of consistently reproducing the "Lusophone world" as a legitimate cultural, social, and political entity – a renewed imperial cartography and epistemology as ongoing project. *The Island of Príncipe* is, in this regard, indicative of the dominant visual renderings of the postcolony within Lusophone circuits of consumption – a type of rendering that resituates Portugal and white bodies as epistemological agents over postcolonial terrains.

São Toméan Filmmakers, Shifting Aesthetics

The last two decades have seen an emergence of São Toméan filmmakers in parallel with strengthened modes of consumption – not only a greater (though incomplete) democratization of television and internet access, but also the opening or reconstruction of theaters in older cinemas and in cultural centers. This growth in national cinematic production and consumption arguably converged in the shape of the annual São Tomé FestFilm: International Film Festival of São Tomé e Príncipe, inaugurated in 2014 which has brought together works – shorts, feature-length films, documentaries, and fiction – from mainly Portuguese-speaking nations, though the number of participating films from other parts of the world has grown in recent editions. Although the festival remains relatively small, it has nonetheless marked an important moment in São Toméan film by providing a forum where national production can be showcased in an international context, while building a national audience.

The 2010s have seen the emergence of new São Toméan filmmakers and a branching out by established ones into diverse sorts of projects. For instance, Januário Afonso, Kalú Mendes, and Caló Costa, produced films during the previous decade for largely pedagogical purposes, mainly in the form of documentaries such as *Água Boa, Vida Saudável* [*Clean Water, Healthy Life*] (2010) and *O Fogo do Apagar da Vida* [*The Fire of Expiring Life*] (2002) on HIV prevention. Afonso, who has established himself as a feature filmmaker on pressing social topics, beginning with *O Fogo*, branched out to different issues and with more complex plots and shot sequences, as in his *O Avesso da Vida*

[*The Reverse of Life*] (2013), which follows the experience of Mr. Albertino, an elderly man left homeless after his daughter places him in a nursery home, thus interrogating the ageist structures of national society and modernity at large.

The beginning of the decade also brought documentaries, as well as fictional works, revisiting histories of colonial oppression and contemporary continuities of colonial structures, from the engineering of São Tomé e Príncipe's labor population in the nineteenth century to contemporary migratory experiences of São Toméans in Europe. Leão Lopes's *Os Últimos Contratados* [*The Last Contract Laborers*] (2010) and Júlio Silvão Tavares' *São Tomé: Minha Terra, Minha Mãe, e Minha Madrasta* [*São Tomé: My Country, My Mother, and My Stepmother*] (2012), to name two of the most relevant, retell the history of migrant labor to the islands from continental Africa and Cabo Verde after the official abolition of the slave trade. Portuguese colonial authorities preyed on economically marginalized former slave and rural populations to attract, or indeed capture, contracted labor for its sugar and cacao plantations in São Tomé e Príncipe. The infrastructural neglect of Cabo Verde from the Portuguese led to a series of fatal famines spawned by drought from the sixteenth to the twentieth centuries, the most fatal of which (those of 1941-43 and 1947-48) were utilized by the Estado Novo to encourage migrant labor to São Tomé. Some of these very migrants and their descendants constitute the subject of these two particular documentaries. Both intertwine interviews with descendants, oral histories, and footage from many aforementioned colonial film productions on São Tomé e Príncipe's *roças*. In this sense, the films endeavor toward a complex historicization project, while centering subalternized voices as agents of historical knowledge and a nuanced vision of the nation as formed via global processes of racial oppression and racialized divisions of labor.

Another prominent São Toméan filmmaker in the nation's contemporary cinema, Ângelo Torres, has dedicated much of his work to laying bare the experiences of São Toméan migrants abroad. His short film, *Kunta* (2007), draws heavily on his own experiences of deep-seated institutional and everyday racism against African migrants, and black bodies more broadly, in Lisbon. His cinematic treatment of São Toméan migration does not present this phenomena through, or as, one particular experience, however. In his documentary, *Aqui a Batalha Yaguajay – Os Sobreviventes* [*Here, the Battle of Yaguajay - Survivors*] (2014), he retraces the migratory experiences, in a vastly different context, of a group of young São Toméans recruited by the MLSTP shortly after independence to study in Cuba. As part of the postcolonial nation-building process, this group was to become part of a national leadership in the ensuing decades. Among this group was Torres himself. The title's reference to a crucial chapter in the Cuban revolution speaks to the MLSTP's commitment to constructing an anti-imperial nation through Global Southern internationalist bonds, as well as the estrangement felt by the São Toméan students while in Cuba and upon return to São Tomé e Príncipe.

Torres's filmography also intervenes in colonial and postcolonial São Toméan historicization, especially in his documentary, *Mionga ki Obô – Mar e Selva* [*Mionga ki Obô – Sea and the Wild*] (2005). The film explores the history and different mythologies surrounding the Angolares people of São Tomé e Príncipe. Colonial rhetoric and historiography argued that the Angolares arrived in São Tomé e Príncipe from northern Angola by way of a shipwreck in the Gulf of Guinea, and that they were among the earliest inhabitants of the islands. The film enacts a postcolonial rehistoricization of the Angolares, that the present-day coastal fishing community did not originate from a shipwreck, but from runaway slaves spanning four centuries. This retelling fundamentally undoes Portuguese accounts, which arguably served to prop up a narrative of nonviolent colonial relations. In doing so, the film also charts a genealogy of anti-colonial resistance at the core of the development of a São Toméan people and nation.

A similar line of production and historical inquiry can be found in *Tchiloli – Identidade de um Povo* [*Tchiloli – the Identity of a People*] (2010), directed by Felisberto Branco, and produced by Kalú Mendes. The film centers on *Tchiloli* – both a São Toméan theatrical piece and a particular approach to theater and performance originating in colonial São Tomé and Príncipe as a form of cultural resistance to Portuguese authority. *Tchiloli* was the São Toméan Creole name given to the production by a local theater company of *Tragédia do Marquês de Mântua e do Imperador Carlos Magno* [*The Tragedy of the Marquis of Mântua and the Emperor Charlemagne*], originally written in the sixteenth century by the Madeiran poet Baltazar Dias. The legacy of the original *tchiloli* continues today with the annual performance of *Auto de Floripes* in numerous communities across the country.

Following one particular theater group's production of the *Tchiloli*, the documentary outlines the history and importance of the *Tchiloli* to an anti-colonial narrative of São Toméan national formation. In this regard, *Tchiloli* has come to stand for a mode of cultural production based on the appropriation and resignification of previous cultural products from both Europe and Africa. As such, the *Tchiloli* is an act of knowing. Regarding São Toméan history and its cultural formation prior to and following colonization, Inocência Mata posits the nation as the result of various cultural encounters between identities and cultural expressions that were also products of dynamic political and cultural forces: 'São Tomé e Príncipe, mestiça nação africana que concilia elementos de culturas já então mestiças quando da sua integração, é o resultado de um doloroso processo transculturativo que prolongou por muitos séculos' ['São

Tomé e Princípe, a *mestizo* African nation that reconciles elements of different cultures that were themselves *mestizo* when integrated, is the result of a painful transcultural process that lasted many centuries'] (Mata 2004, 18). In the sphere of cinematic consumption, the aforementioned films by Branco, Torres, and Lopes on histories of migration and quotidian forms of anti-imperial postcolonial resistance intertwine and produce a particular subaltern knowledge of long-durée imperialism and its discursive and institutional fabrics across spaces, while also imagining forms of anti-imperial freedom.

Emerging Filmmakers and Media in the late 2010s

The aforementioned festival, São Tomé FestFilm, as well as internet-based media and the expansion of television consumption have provided new platforms for the emergence of a new generation of São Toméan filmmakers in the later-half of the 2010s, including women and young filmmakers without access to production houses and connections to public and private entities for financial support. The festival has thus also provided a platform for young São Toméan filmmakers to debut their films. For instance, the 2018 edition saw three such filmmakers screen their debut short films: Valeri André Menezes with his *Quem é o teu parceiro?* [*Who is your partner?*], Juelce Beija Flor with his *Filhos D'agua* [*Children of Water*], and Kátia Aragão with her *Mina Kiá* [*Little Maid*]. While becoming one of the first female filmmakers garnering national and international attention (her film has also featured in other Lusophone film festivals), particularly after winning the prize for best national short film at the 2018 FestFilm, Aragão has centered structural and intersectional oppression along with gender and class in ways that have been less than prominent in postcolonial São Toméan film.

Mina Kiá follows the life of Tónia, a young girl residing with her parents in a rural village, but sent to live with her aunt and uncle in São Tomé city where she is forced to work as a housemaid for her relatives while also enduring physical abuse and sexual violence. The story, portraying gendered and geo-economic structures of labor, oppression, and exploitability, is nonetheless not merely one of monolithic victimhood. Rather, Tónia holds firm to her dream of becoming a journalist and pushes forth with her studies despite the abuses she suffers in the home of her relatives. In this regard, *Mina Kiá* is one of the first São Toméan films featuring a rural female protagonist to garner attention, while also developing said protagonist with a degree of complexity corresponding to the challenges of resisting patriarchal systems and oppressive economies of desire.

Aragão, born in 1986, is also representative of an emerging era in São Toméan (and global) film and media, whereby cultural producers of the 2010s have made use of integrated media platforms to extend their voices in the public sphere and movement of cultural products. Through her social media presence, she has not only been able to publicize her work and the venues where it is screened, but also connect and contextualize her work within national, transnational, and Pan-African cultural and activist movements. For instance, her Instagram account features posters of her own screenings, but significantly more content promoting connections with musicians such as Kampire from Uganda, Valete from Portugal (of São Toméan background), other filmmakers, and highlighting events that foster these sorts of connections. Aragão thus situates herself and her work in broader terrains of African cultural production and creators, especially when these connections take place in São Tomé e Príncipe. Given the limited industry and forums for São Toméan filmmakers in the spheres of national cultural production, with significantly less public attention garnered for film than for music and literature, Aragão, through her own forging of public life, has established productive and consumptive networks of national and transnational creative work. In this sense, Aragão positions herself in public life as both producer and consumer; a curator of cultural production in which she embeds her own works, through online life, and in working with different organizations and initiatives to create spaces for cultural production and producers in São Tomé e Príncipe.

Other young São Toméan filmmakers have found social media to be their primary forum of dissemination, existing as a dominant platform of consumption as internet access expands in São Tomé e Príncipe. Such a platform is particularly relevant to consumers of globally circulating products of popular culture, where access is enhanced and, subsequently, consumptive tastes are negotiated. With such an audience in mind, amateur filmmakers have found a niche for themselves with film genres including horror and crime that have been historically dismissed in African and Third World filmmaking circles as western capitalist aesthetics incapable of representing struggle and society from the periphery of the world system. Despite low production budgets and amateur shooting and editing, such films have garnered significant viewerships, intertwining in complex ways with youth cultures in São Tomé e Príncipe, spanning music and fashion. One such filmmaker, Aguinaldo Carvalho, director and screenwriter of at least three films, has worked with a local production start-up, BNK Best Movies, which has been dedicated to producing and disseminating content in both film and music (namely Hip-Hop and Kizomba), also creating award shows for young São Toméan cultural producers. By having his films inserted into youth markets and through accessible platforms of consumption such as YouTube and Facebook, Carvalho has gained a large following considering the fragmentary history of São Toméan cinema. His first film, *Viagem sem Volta* [*Journey of No*

Return] (2017), reached over 15,000 views on YouTube, as of June 2020; a significant portion of the country's population of 204,000.

The horror film, made up exclusively of young São Toméan actors, is geared toward a similar national demographic, with the soundtrack featuring recording artists produced through BNK. The plot follows a group of young adults who venture into a forest for a camping trip, but quickly become the target of a mysterious killer who lives in the forest. Aside from *Viagem sem Volta*'s sequel, Carvalho also directed the short film, *Jogos Ilegais* [*Illicit Games*] (2018), the second of his filmography, representing an experimental shift from the horror genre to urban crime – another globally-circulating and popular genre among young São Toméans. The film's plot, similar to many others of the genre, didactically highlights the perils of gang life on the urban margins, centering on a young São Toméan male protagonist who gets involved with a local São Tomé city street gang. He is ultimately dissuaded from continuing to partake in the gang by a middle-aged father figure. Despite the film's significantly smaller viewership of 3,100 (as of June 2020) when compared to *Viagem sem Volta*, the film represents an attempt to tap into, or create, a young São Toméan urban audience that is connected to social media, popular culture, and the technologies through which these are consumed.

While films such as Kátia Aragão's *Mina Kiá*, or those of Kalú Mendes and Ângelo Torres explored above, have featured on the film festival circuit and disseminated to a particular Lusophone international audience, Aguinaldo Carvalho's films reveal a different cinematic audience. This is one of perhaps more casual consumption in which São Toméan film is intertwined with popular visual and audio cultures. Despite possible problems and shortcomings, this young São Toméan audience must be considered an important part of contemporary and future São Toméan cinema.

Conclusion

The trajectory of São Toméan cinema cannot be separated from colonial history and the long-durée of empire. The São Toméan filmmakers covered above, from Januário Afonso to Aguinaldo Carvalho, have all grappled in different ways with the legacies of Portuguese colonialism and postcolonial realities in late capitalism. There continues to be a struggle faced by São Toméan filmmakers to convey national realities independently from international funding. Despite emerging aesthetics, São Toméan film continues to be ensnared in neocolonial and late capitalist webs of economic flows and paternalist narratives framed around "development" held by international agencies. Such financiers, in other words, have largely funded productions from the Global South that can be considered aesthetics of "underdevelopment." Kátia Aragão's *Mina Kiá*, for instance, as a recent example, was funded by the European External Action Service of the European Union. In this regard, there is transformative potential in a young São Toméan audience that is interested in films not framed around images of underdevelopment, despite low production budgets. This signals a popular interest in consuming images of São Toméan realities that do not essentialize life in the periphery of the world system through frameworks of poverty. Rather than presenting societal life on the margins of globalization, Aguinaldo Carvalho's films present a generation that is in tune with and participating in negotiations of global popular culture while carving out a place for São Tomé e Príncipe and African visual cultural production within it.

Works Cited

A Colónia de Moçambique. Directed by Fernandes Thomaz. Brigada Cinematográfica Portuguesa. 1931.

A cultura do Cacau. Directed by Ernesto de Albuquerque. Empresa Internacional de Cinematografia. 1909.

Água Boa, Vida Saudável. Directed by Kalú Mendes. KM Produções. 2010.

A Ilha do Príncipe: O Éden Esquecido do Atlântico. Directed by João Teles de Vasconcelos. Aidnature. 2014.

Andrade-Watkins, Claire. "Portuguese African Cinema: Historical and Contemporary Perspectives: 1969-1993. *Research in African Literatures*. Vol 26, No. 3. pp. 134-150. 1995. Print.

Aqui a Batalha Yaguajay – Os Sobreviventes. Directed by Angelo Torres. Cinemate. 2014.

Arenas, Fernando. *Lusophone Africa: Beyond Independence*. Minneapolis, MN: University of Minnesota Press, 2011.

As Ilhas Crioulas de Cabo Verde. António Lopes Ribeiro. Missão Cinematográfica às Colónias Africanas. 1945.

Castelo, Claudia. *Passagens para África*. Lisbon: Edições Afrontamento. 2007. Print.

Catembe. Directed by M. G. Faria de Almeida. Sociedade Portuguesa de Actualidades Cinematográficas. 1965.

Comunidade Luso-Brasileira. António Lopes Ribeiro. Missão Cinematográfica às Colónias Africanas. 1958.

Curto, Diogo. *O Colonialismo Português em África - De Livingstone a Luandino*. Lisbon, Portugal: Edições 70, 1959.

De Lisboa a São Tomé. Directed by António Antunes Mata and José César de Sá. Brigada Cinematográfica Portuguesa. 1933.

Extra Bitter: Tthe Legacy of the Chocolate Islands. Directed by Derek Vertongen. Filmakers Library. 2000.

Gentes que Nós Civilizamos. António Lopes Ribeiro. Missão Cinematográfica às Colónias Africanas. 1944.

Falconi, Jessica and Kamila Krakowska. "Panorama do Cinema e do Audiovisual em São Tomé e Príncipe." *Revista Mulemba*. Vol 9, No. 17. pp. 177-193. 2017.

Feitiço do Império. António Lopes Ribeiro. Missão Cinematográfica às Colónias Africanas. 1940.

Instituto Marquês de Valle Flôr. "Estatutos do Instituto Marquês de Vale Flor, que se refere o Decreto no. 38:351, de 1 de Agosto de 1951." https://www.imvf.org/wp-content/uploads/2018/02/1a.pdf. Accessed: August 4, 2019.

Jogos Ilegais. Directed by Aguinaldo Carvalho. BNK Best. 2018.

Kunta. Directed by Ângelo Torres. Blablabla Media. 2007.

Little Fruit: At the Equator Everything is Possible. Directed by Herbert Brödl. Baumhaus Film Brödl. 1998.

Mata, Inocência. *A Suave Pátria: Reflexões Político-Culturais Sobre a Sociedade São-Tomense.* Lisboa: Edições Colibri, 2004.

Matos, Patrícia Ferraz de. "Imagens de África? Filmes e Documentários Portugueses Relativos às Antigas Colónias Africanas (Primeira Metade do Século XX)." *Comunicação e Sociedade*, vol 29. pp. 153-174.

Mina Kiá. Directed by Katya Aragão. Tela Digital Media Group. 2017.

Mionga ki Obô – Mar e Selva. Directed by Angelo Torres. Lx Filmes. 2005.

Mortu Nega. Directed by Flora Gomes. Instituto Nacional de Cinema de Guiné Bissau. 1988.

Nossos Irmãos, os Africans. Directed by Ed Keffel. Sociedade Dom Pedro II. 1963.

O Avesso da Vida. Directed by Januário Afonso. KM Produções. 2013.

O Cacau Escravo e Trabalho Indígena em S. Tomé. Directed by Cardoso Furtado. Geographical Society of Lisbon. 1909.

O Fogo do Apagar da Vida. Directed by Januário Afonso. KM Produções. 2002.

Os Últimos Contratados. Directed by Leão Lopes. 2010.

Por Terras de Ébano. Directed by Augusto Seara. Agência Geral do Ultramar. 1929.

"Portugal e o regime do trabalho indígena nas suas colónias" (No author). Lisboa: Imprensa Nacional. 1910.

São Tomé Agrícola e Industrial. Directed by Augusto Seara. Agência Geral do Ultramar. 1929.

São Tomé: Minha Terra, Minha Mãe, e Minha Madrasta. Directed by Júlio Silvão Tavares. Silvão Produções. 2012.

Segunda Viagem Triunfal. António Lopes Ribeiro. Missão Cinematográfica às Colónias Africanas. 1940.

Solanas, Fernando and Octavio Gettino. "Hacia un Tercer Cine." *Tricontinental* 13. 1969. Print. manifesto, "Towards a Third Cinema."

Taylor, Clyde. "Film Reborn in Mozambique." *Jumpcut* 28. pp. 30-31. 1983.

Tchiloli – Identidade de um Povo. Directed by Felisberto Branco and Kalú Mendes. KM Produções. 2010.

Terra Mãe. Directed by Augusto Fraga. Sociedade Portuguesa de Actualidades Cinematográficas. 1960.

Udju Azul di Yonta. Directed by Flora Gomes. Instituto Nacional de Cinema de Guiné Bissau. 1992.

Uma Visita às Propriedades da Sociedade Agrícola Valle Flor. Directed by Augusto Seara. Brigada Cinematográfica Portuguesa. 1929.

Viagem do Chefe de Estado às Colónias de Angola e São Tomé e Príncipe. António Lopes Ribeiro. Missão Cinematográfica às Colónias Africanas. 1939.

Viagem Sem Volta. Directed by Aguinaldo Carvalho. BNK Best. 2017.

Vieira, Patrícia. "Fetish Empire as the New State: Spell Empire and the Colonial Sortilégio." *Portuguese Cultural Studies* 3.1. pp. 126-144. 2010.

Chapter 6

The Orphan as Post-colonial Allegory in Lusophone African Film: *A Cidade Vazia* and *Republica di Mininus*

Patrícia Martinho Ferreira

University of Massachusetts Amherst

Abstract

Many Lusophone African feature films engage with the representation of orphans and the ways in which they either succumb to their social and political environment or have to adapt to it. Through an analysis of Hollow City (2004) by Maria João Ganga and Republica di Mininus (2012) by Flora Gomes, I juxtapose a tragic trajectory of loss with a trajectory of redemption. Ganga's pessimistic view of Luanda's urban space, derived from the emptiness of societal values and the lack of good role models, contrasts with Gomes's optimistic reinvention of society. The destruction and emptiness portrayed in Republica de Mininus are seen as inevitable to a much-desired rebirth of postcolonial African societies. This paper argues that Gomes' utopian project is rooted in a positive and transformative view of orphanhood, whereas Ganga's defeatist project conceives of the state of being an orphan as fatal.

Keywords: orphan; war; loss; redemption; Maria João Ganga, Flora Gomes

* * *

Introduction: On the Concept of the Orphan

The orphan has been used in literature to express a wide range of ideas. In fact, various studies present the orphan as a flexible literary trope, capable of shedding light on the anxieties of the historical eras in which such a character is depicted. According to William Floyd, the orphan has the potential to metamorphose into and/or to embody cultural affairs: "the orphan is often a register of cultural concerns, his or her state speaking to various societal anxieties and predicaments in ways as numerous as the orphan's different incarnations" (Floyd 2011, 56). Eva König comes to a similar conclusion when analyzing the orphan's recurrence in eighteenth century English fiction: "the orphan represents the characteristic anxieties of his age and contributions to the ideological creation of the new bourgeois subject" (König 2014, 4). In König's view, the orphan emerges mainly at a metaphorical level and functions as a cryptogram: "a useful trope for novelists to think about what it means to become a subject, what conditions are attached to the social place that an individual can claim, or under what circumstances that social place can be changed" (König 2014, 242). Furthermore, orphaned characters can be characterized in a dual manner, either the orphan is seen as an outcast who should be banned from society or as a fragile member of society who needs to be fully protected. In either case, "orphans are clearly marked as being different from the rest of society. They are the eternal Other" (Kimball 1999, 559).

A few critics have observed that, in fiction, orphans symbolize tragedy, demonstrating a dual nature, that is, they can provoke sympathy and compassion, but at the same time contempt, they can symbolize hope, but also despair. The orphan, thus described, is leading a life free from parental interference and restrictions, but s/he is deprived of the freedom and privileges of a so-called normal child. In *The Orphan: A Journey to Wholeness*, Audrey Punnett clearly reiterates this duality, stating: "The orphan stands alone and has on the one hand a potential for growth and new beginnings, and on the other hand, the potential for remaining isolated and on the outside" (Punnett 2014, 22). In literary history there are several legendary orphans, and they often earn the epithet of the hero due to their resilience and wit in face of adversity. They are self-contained and lead a fascinating life of adventurers in search of affection, identity and success.

If the concept of the orphan has been extensively examined in studies on eighteenth and nineteenth centuries English literature, works on orphanhood in twentieth and twenty-first centuries literary production have already begun to emerge. In a volume on contemporary American literature, Maria Troy, Elizabeth Kella and Helena Wahlström explore the connections between national crisis and orphanhood, stating, on the one hand, that the figure of the orphan abounds in American literature, and, on the other hand, that this figure almost always emerges in times when the family and the national identity are in crisis, being related to processes of "scapegoating, displacement, and marginalization" (Troy 2014, 2). The volume here follows the core ideas of several other works on this subject. For instance, Valerie Loichot (2007) puts forward the idea that the orphan is an active element in the reconstruction of the family narrative in the context of post-slavery America and the French Caribbean; Carol Singley (2011) analyzes literary representations of forms of "adoption" in works by American writers, showing how the orphaned figure underlines the historical evolution of the idea of an "American nation." Additionally, studies of the orphan in the postcolonial context stand out. Julin Everett (2009), for example, seeks to analyze the orphan's autobiographical writing in two Jamaican novels; Motoko Sugano (2009) sees the orphan as a figure of resistance to colonial discourse in works by Australian authors who rewrite Charles Dickens' *Great Expectations*; and, based on the metaphors of exile, dismemberment, limbo and orphanhood, Sara Gusky (2014) explores the legacy of violence in the Caribbean, a context in which the orphan does not appear as a victim, but as an active element, capable of creating new kinship and community ties, which the author calls "fictive kinship." Lastly, mention should be made of Ludovic Obiang's reflections on the context of contemporary African cultures and, in particular, the role of traditional tales. This author examines the idea of malleability and ambivalence associated with the trope of the orphan, but at the same time disputes the long-established positive view of it. In Obiang's view, the orphan can translate unpromising and hopeless environments: "au contraire du roman moderne, nous semble-t-il, la condition précaire et pitoyable de l'orphelin traduit la misère et la désolation ambiantes, l'univers labyrinthique et apocalyptique dans lequel ce dernier est plonge" (Obiang 2002, 207).

In film studies, the trope of the orphan has also acquired relevant meanings that go hand in hand with those identified in works of literary criticism. In particular, Constantin Parvulescu's analysis of Soviet cinema has shown how the orphan exposes the concerns of the political apparatus. In the works analyzed by the author, the cinematic trope of the orphan serves to interrogate the Eastern Europe socialist system's shortcomings as well as the post-World War II historical context, during which the number of orphans was high and the values of the traditional family were at stake. As maintained by Parvulescu,

> The figure of the orphan was also instrumental in advertising and investigating alternative and superior social bonds (superior to those of the traditional family), but also in approaching individual trauma, loss, memory and rebellion. The orphan enabled films to explore the role of family ties and both individual and social alienation. (Parvulescu 2015, 3)

Informed by the critical framework around the concept of orphanhood, I claim that the dual role (despair vs. hope; fragility vs. resilience; etc.) allowed by the flexible and symbolic nature of the orphan can also be found in Lusophone African cinema. I specifically argue that the representation of the orphan is central to the overall understanding of many films that (dys)utopically problematize the complexities of contemporary Lusophone African societies marked by colonialism, the struggle for independence and the post-independence wars, which have killed, displaced and impoverished millions of people, including children. Having this in mind, Parvulescu's argument regarding the orphan's role in the Soviet cinema can be applied *mutatis mutandis* to the Lusophone context. The orphans become "a symbolic figure that gestured at the same time toward the traumatic experience of the war, the guilt of participating in it, and the hope of rebuilding civilization." In this sense, they embody "a continent in search of new forms of political parenthood, promising itself not to repeat the mistakes of the past" (Parvulescu 2015, 3-4).

As a matter of fact, the orphan characters in Lusophone African cinema allow for a rich reflection on the postcolonial period, whether these characters appear in film adaptions, such as *Terra Sonâmbula* (2007) by Teresa Prata[1] (based on Mia Couto's novel with the same title), or in original scripts such as *A Cidade Vazia* (2004) by Maria João Ganga[2] and *Republica di Mininus* (2012) by Flora Gomes.[3] These films bear witness to the confusing and violent post-independent period and the disastrous aftermath of the civil wars in Mozambique, Angola and Guinea-Bissau respectively. The literal representations of the orphans highlight either the ways in which these orphans succumb to their social and political environment or successfully adapt to it or even fight to change it. Through a comparative analysis of two films *A Cidade Vazia* and *Republica di Mininus*, I juxtapose a tragic trajectory of despair and loss of innocence set during the context of Angola's civil war with a trajectory of redemption and hope set in the context of another African country devastated by war. Even though Gomes seems to have the reality of Guinea-Bissau in mind, this film goes beyond national borders, pointing to a broader perspective on social and political challenges experienced in many African countries. *Terra Sonâmbula* will not be considered for this paper given that it deals with the specificities of film adaptation, whereas the other two films are original scripts.

---

[1] Teresa Prata was born in Portugal and spent her childhood in Mozambique. She studied biology at the University of Coimbra and holds a degree in Screenwriting and Directing from the German Film and Television School. She began her career working at an art gallery and has made several experimental videos and installations. Terra Sonâmbula (Sleepwalking Land) is her first feature film.

[2] Maria João Ganga was born in Huambo, Angola, in 1964. She studied filmmaking at L'École Superieure Libre d'Etudes Cinematographiques (ESEC) in Paris. She has served as an assistant director on several documentaries, including Rostov-Luanda by Abderrahmane Sissako, and has also written and directed for theater.

[3] Flora Gomes was born in Cadique, Guinea-Bissau in 1949. He studied cinematography at the Cuban Film Institute (ICAC), returning to West Africa to work as a journalist and to learn newsreel production under Paulin Soumanou Vieyra, the late Beninese/Senegalese filmmaker.

A Cidade Vazia or a Dystopian View of Angola's Post-colonial Society

After 13 years of Colonial War/Independence War (1961-1974), Angola's 27-year civil war can be roughly divided into three periods of major fighting, from 1975 to 1991, 1992 to 1994 and 1998 to 2002, with short and fragile periods of peace. By the time the MPLA achieved victory in 2002, more than half a million people had died and over one million had been internally displaced. These wars destroyed Angola's infrastructure and severely damaged public administration, the economy, and social and religious institutions. According to the non-governmental organization *SOS Children's Villages*, during the Angolan civil war an estimated 700,000 children lost either one or both of their parents.[4] The protagonist of *A Cidade Vazia* portrays the life of one of these many orphans. As the film was completed almost fifteen years after Ganga began writing the script and released only two years after the final peace agreement between MPLA and UNITA,[5] one can understand why there is no space for a utopian view in this film. Indeed, the overall message conveyed by the destiny of the orphan protagonist is that of frustration with the dynamics of the postcolonial period, and more particularly with Luanda's urban environment, marked by scarcity, poverty, violence, and crime. The protagonist's trajectory can be considered a coming-of-age story with an unfortunate and inauspicious end. His loss of innocence, set during the context of Angola's long civil war, presents no hope to the audience who follows his perspective since the beginning of the film. The various close-ups of the young protagonist may be interpreted as an obvious invitation to empathy.

After seeing his family massacred by soldiers in his village of the province of Bié, located in the central part of the country, 11-year-old Ndala, along with a group of other orphans, is airlifted to Luanda by Catholic missionaries. At the airport, hoping to make his way back home, Ndala slips away from the nuns. As he wanders the streets bewildered by traffic and noise, a group of children at school rehearses a play about a young heroic soldier named Ngunga. This hero's perseverance, despite his fear and the pain of his wounds, becomes a metaphor for Ndala's experience in the city. The director strategically uses the schoolchildren's staging of *As aventuras de Ngunga*, a novel by the Angolan writer Pepetela published in 1973,[6] as a *mise en scene*-like device in reverse to

---

[4] https://www.sos-childrensvillages.org/

[5] As Carolin Overhoff Ferreira notes: "Her project dated from 1991, but given the political situation, could not be turned into reality until after the end of the war." (2012, p. 155).

[6] As Aventuras de Ngunga tells the story of a boy who learns self-reliance through his experiences as a guerrilla fighter. Pepetela (1941-) has been called a "guerrilla-writer" – he was a strong supporter of the nationalists in the war fought for Angolan independence. N'gunga, the protagonist, suffers the colonial violence, his parents are killed the

draw a stark comparison between the young Ngunga's formation as a revolutionary and patriot, and the neglect and exploitation of the film's protagonist. The choice of this powerful intertext clearly reinforces Ndala's tragic path. And, in this way, instead of being granted hope for the future, the audience is confronted with a spiral of misfortunes that leads to Ndala's death.

In other words, *A Cidade Vazia* juxtaposes, with striking effect, two historical periods: the impassioned period of the Angolan fight for Independence, and the all-pervading turmoil that ensued after it. The two children, Ngunga and Ndala, represent the two time periods – one of great expectations and the other of a ruthless reality. In the 70s, Ngunga is a symbol of the revolutionary times. He is a brave child, aware of the need to change the world and raise the level of consciousness in adults. In the early 90s, Ndala, a war orphan and refugee, is dragged into a world with no future, dominated by unspeakable violence and the struggle for survival. Ngunga is fearful and gradually becomes fearless, as he learns to navigate a path toward adulthood. Ndala is fearless and gradually becomes fearful, as he is enmeshed in Luanda's urban environment. In the rehearsal scenes, Ngunga is injured and upset, and his fellow actors tell him to have courage ("a man must never be afraid" – the young actor says); the scene is unresolved when it ends, but the audience imagines a positive conclusion to the events. By contrast, Ndala grows stronger every day in his resolution to return to Bié, but what the audience also sees are the numerous dangers posed by Luanda's cityscape and the complex dynamics of the new family of "cousins" and "sisters" he has gained through his friendship with Zé – the 13-year-old boy who plays Ngunga and dreams about being a real actor. Not by chance, these two plot lines overlap explicitly at the end, as the play is performed in parallel to the robbery during which Ndala ends up dying.

Without his parents and freed from the rules of the missionaries, Ndala is ready to begin his journey, exploring the city. It is worth noting that in the panoramic scene of Luanda the camera is behind Ndala, granting the audience an ample view of the city but, above all, of the vulnerability of the young boy facing it. Also relevant are the instrumental sounds and the close-up that follows of a mentally disturbed vagrant looking for food in a trash bin. This bizarrely long close-up anticipates the following scenes of a chaotic city with shortages of water and food. Ndala's curiosity will make him keep crossing paths with Zé, who introduces him to Ngunga's adventures, the excitement of the cinema, and, later on, to adult behaviors and activities, such as listening to

---

Portuguese soldiers in the fight for independence. This novel deals with several themes: utopia and national liberation, political consciousness, importance of the school and education in the projection of a better and new future, among others.

music, dancing, smoking, drinking and having sex. It is also Zé who introduces Ndala to Rosita, who gives Ndala a place to stay in return for doing chores, and to Joka, whose confidence fascinates Ndala.

Ndala's path as an orphan is established right from the first scene in which he appears. Ndala is the only child who looks out of the window while being airlifted, suggesting both his spirit of curiosity and his attentiveness, while also symbolizing the loss of family and home. As the audience later learns, he is leaving his land behind and looking at the sky where he believes his family now lives, as the nuns had taught about the afterlife. His desire to return to Bié is not only shared with Zé but also with the old fisherman who gives him shelter in his shack at the beach and tells him stories about the Goddess Kianda, a key figure in Angolan mythology. The act of looking back has a tragic meaning, particularly in the scene of Ndala's death, right after he is compelled by Joka to shoot at the man whose house they have broken into. In shock at having killed the man, Ndala goes back to stare at the painting on the wall, which reminds him of the Tchokwe mask used in the ceremony performed by his family on the night they were killed. The flashback of the destruction of Ndala's village gains, in this ending sequence, a symbolic meaning: like the ceremony, Ndala's life (his passage from childhood to adulthood) is tragically disrupted. The long close-up of Ndala's face, intensified by the sound of the saxophone playing in a minor key, reveals a deep sadness and the anticipation of his death. Cinematographically, this final sequence is superbly done. The image of the spiral staircase connects with the eyes of the painted masquerade, and both of these elements dialogue with the spinning propeller of the aircraft that had transported Ndala to Luanda, the place where he will die. Furthermore, the closing song emphasizes the complete lack of hope for the displaced and orphan children, like the obedient and innocent Ndala, echoing the vacuum, the disillusionment of the political project which had as its core value, supposedly, the good of the nation. The lyrics could not be more straightforward: "generation of pain, eternal beggars (…) precocious children sailing without reaching the sea of hope." This song clearly attests to the fact that the hopes of the fights for independence have not come true. The serious repercussions of the war and lack of governance in Angola is expressed by many Angolan novelists and poets. Ana Paula Tavares' poem "November without water", published in 1999, also clearly conveys the level of suffering lived by "generation of pain":

> Olha-me p'ra estas crianças de vidro
> cheias de água até às lágrimas
> enchendo a cidade de estilhaços
> procurando a vida
> nos caixotes do lixo.

Olha-me estas crianças transporte
animais de carga sobre os dias
percorrendo a cidade até aos bordos
carregam a morte sobre os ombros
despejam-se sobre o espaço
enchendo a cidade de estilhaços.
(Tavares 1999, 36)[7]

The mismatch between Ndala and Zé, his true friend, that happens by mid-film enables Ndala's downfall, as it allows him to look up to Joka as a model of masculinity. Joka steals various supplies from the city and sells them to the community. He has a car, and girls, and he carries himself with a sense of confidence and dominance. It is clear that Ndala is fascinated by Joka, the way he looks and the world he embodies. He aspires to be strong and to have Joka's life, even though he doesn't know much about him. He even tells Joka, "When I grow up, I want to be like you." Joka replies, "A mechanic?" And Ndala answers back, "No. Strong, like you." In this scene, Joka actually tries to convince Ndala that being a kid is much better than being an adult, but Ndala doesn't seem to agree, as he wants to be grown-up like Joka someday. What is tragically hinted very early on is that the relationship with Joka eventually leads Ndala to a death end: Joka realizes how valuable Ndala's height is and convinces him to break into a house to help him to conduct a robbery during which Ndala ends up dying.

With his own life at stake, Ndala cannot see the danger before it has overtaken him. He is an obedient boy who is forced to experience life in Luanda: begging, working in the streets, smoking, drinking, and eventually robbing and killing. After losing his hope to return to Bié, he succumbs to Luanda, described as "a jungle" by both the nun and Zé, the ones who selflessly care for Ndala by advising him and thus protecting him from the multiple dangers of the city. One notes that Ndala's downfall becomes predictable after the bullying scene in which Ndala is selling Rosita's cigars in a zone ruled by a group of boys who see him as an intruder. The "jungle" has its own rules and Ndala is not able, as the nun foresees, to understand and survive it. Moreover, the protagonist's

---

[7] My translation of this song is literal and does not aim to represent the poetic dimension of Tavares' language: "Just look at these children of glass / full of water right up to their tears / filling the city with shrapnel pieces / searching for life / in garbage bins. / / Just look at these transport children / beasts of burden over the days / roaming the city to its borders / bearing death on their shoulders / spilling themselves over space / filling the city with shrapnel pieces."

tragedy is inscribed in his own name – according to Ganga, Ndala is a frequent name in the province of Bié and translates as "the one who is marked."[8] The word Ndala can also refer to palm branches that stand as a symbol of triumph and hope, which is highly ironic given that Ndala is not victorious at all.

The process of social adaptation in many orphans' trajectories requires cutting ties with the past in order to envision a new kinship system that eventually will allow the orphan to succeed. But this is not the case in *A Cidade Vazia*. The audience follows Ndala as he hopes to return to Bié and at the same time makes an effort to accept his new life and reality. The viewer is shown, however, that Ndala's innocent and obedient nature prevents him from fully understanding the city's dynamics, which are based on a committed struggle for survival at all costs – Rosita's indifference to the young victims of the war, the lack of solidarity of the boys selling merchandise and cigars in the streets, and Joka's harmfulness as a role model are examples of the pervasive violence that characterized the Angolan post-independence period of civil war. The irony behind the character's name points to the dual nature of some orphan trajectories that Kimball and others have identified. Ndala is clearly a fragile member of the society who needs protection and whose curious mind and resilient spirit are betrayed by the "kinship" he forms in Luanda. The lack of parents, to impose limits, doesn't help Ndala to be free and adventurous; on the contrary, Ndala's tragedy results from the complete lack of orientation and affection. Focused only on his material success, Joka uses Ndala rather than protecting him.

In an overarching interpretation, *A Cidade Vazia* stands out as a dystopian representation of an entire generation: the generation that fought against the colonial power and dragged itself into a cruel fratricidal war, responsible for the high number of orphaned children in the country. Angola's civil war is a national wound and the expressive adjective of the title encapsulates this national tragedy. According to Carolin Overhoff Ferreira, "The emptiness referred to in the title stems from the obligatory retreat at night, but serves at the same time as a metaphor for the complete lack of values in Angola's society" (Ferreira, 2012 155).

Republica di Mininus or a Manifesto for an Ethical Revolution

Having grown up during colonialism in Guinea-Bissau and participated in the fight against its oppressive and unjust colonial system, it is undeniable that Flora Gomes' filmography conveys his disillusionment regarding the postcolonial period that did not bring the anticipated peace and economic prosperity to his

---

[8] See https://www.afrik.com/quand-le-cinema-angolais-renait.

country. The development of Guinea-Bissau has been impossible to bring forth, due to several military coups, unstable governments,[9] and a deep culture of corruption (very often carried out by lobbying groups called *tchutchiduris*) that permeates all levels of social and political power, including the judiciary, and surfaces as an undeniable effect of the colonial enterprise (especially in what concerns the centralization of power). According to António Soares Lopes, "Tráfico de armas, narcotráfico, perseguições, intrigas, prisões e assassinatos fazem parte do dia-a-dia do país que Amílcar Cabral um dia idealizou como terra de paz e de progresso, a terra do 'homem novo'" (Lopes 2015, 94).[10]

Confronted with a social reality marked by mismanagement, the absence of a collective interest, the abandonment of the population's well-being, violent military coups, poverty, inequality, ambition, and the violation of human rights, Gomes resists by emphasizing the potential of the younger generation. In fact, Gomes refuses to dig in the past (in several interviews, the director has asserted that he is not interested in looking at the past), instead he adopts a transformative perspective, projecting new possibilities, as if saying that what is missing in Guinea-Bissau's society are ideas with the potential to lead to new actions. He follows the school of the Senegalese Ousmane Sembène, the pioneer of African cinema, who holds that films should be able to teach and inspire, following the classic notion that art ought to educate and entertain.[11]

One of the most esteemed directors in Lusophone Africa, Gomes aims to overcome the ethnographic depiction of Africa created by the Europeans, the image of an idyllic paradise, while also eschewing images of war, destruction and poverty. His work has been characterized by "eclecticism in aesthetic approaches and ambivalence towards realist narrative, as well as by Marxist

---

[9] "A instabilidade cíclica reinante da Guiné-Bissau tem números e eles são preocupantes: de 1974 a 2015 o país já teve 14 presidentes e 23 primeiros ministros. Em 40 anos de independência da Guiné-Bissau, apenas três dos dez presidentes e ex-presidentes estão vivos e dois deles afastados da política." ("Guinea-Bissau's cyclical instability has numbers and they are worrying: from 1974 to 2015 the country already had 14 presidents and 23 prime ministers. In 40 years of Guinea-Bissau's independence, only three of the ten presidents and former-presidents are alive and two of them are removed from politics." Lopes, 2015, p. 96, my translation).

[10] "Arms trafficking, drug trafficking, persecutions, intrigues, arrests and murders are part of the daily life of the country that Amílcar Cabral once idealized as the land of peace and progress, the land of the 'new man'" (my translation).

[11] In a 1995 interview with the film scholar Frank Ukadike, Flora Gomes has explicitly declared his deep gratitude and admiration for Ousmane Sembène. See: Ukadike, N. Frank. "In Guinea-Bissau, cinema trickles down: an interview with Flora Gomes." *Research in African Literatures* (1995, Vol. 26 Issue 3, p179-185).

ideological positionings" (Arenas 2011, 119). Critics, such as Jusciele Oliveira and Akin Adesokan, among others, agree that so far all films by Gomes have been guided by an important inquiry: Once Independence has been gained, what can serve as a unifying vision for society in order to achieve a balance between modernization, tradition, social justice, democratization, and environmental sustainability? Exploring local stories with a global resonance is one of the characteristics of Gomes' films, as Jusciele Oliveira points out:

> Os filmes do realizador bissau-guineense Flora Gomes contam histórias locais com desdobramentos globais, já que falam de trânsitos, de música, de mulher, de crianças, de guerra, de neocolonialismo, de cosmogonia, de vida, de morte, de amor, de nascimento, de migração, de tradição, de modernidade, de coletividade, de política. Seus filmes também tratam de problemas socioeconômicos relacionados com o ecossistema (desmatamento, seca, água). (Oliveira 2019, 18)[12]

Transforming and adapting the past to the present circumstances, in a consistent effort to find a middle ground between nostalgia and a nihilist view of the past, seems to be the condition *sine qua non* for the fulfillment of new forms of governance. As Ana Mafalda Leite states, "Flora Gomes seeks to create alternative discourses for imagining the future of Africa and his country" (Leite 2019, 8). In what concerns *Republica di Mininus*, I argue that Gomes's artistic effort is built through the trope of children without parents or adults around them. In this film, orphanhood, resulting from the numerous periods of war that have aggravated the country's instability, is seen as the only way to build a society in which all members must have a voice and the power must be distributed effectively. Hence, orphanhood in this film is deeply intertwined with ideas of enlightenment and reeducation, but, most of all, with ideas of redemption and having a second chance. In this context, Constantin Parvulescu's observations on the Hungarian film *Somewhere in Europe* can shed light on *Republica di Mininus*: "it imagines its orphans as creating a vital and redemptive form of community that, imprinted by the violence of the war, can organize itself spontaneously into a vigorous and dynamic democracy without needing the paternalistic control of organized political apparatuses" (Parvulescu 2015, 6). If, in the case of the Hungarian film, the Communist Party is the political force that should be disputed, in Gomes' film what is at stake are

---

[12] "The films by the Bissau-Guinean director Flora Gomes tell local stories with global developments, as they talk about transits, music, women, children, war, neocolonialism, cosmogony, life, death, love, birth, migration, tradition, modernity, collectivity, politics. His films also address socioeconomic problems related to the ecosystem (deforestation, drought, water)." (my translation).

the dynamics of the neocolonial system, its lasting economic, social and political effects, war and corruption being its worst consequences. Furthermore, what should be totally rejected is the adult's mindset and vicious behaviors. The travelling shot showing the urban space free of adults, right after the five victims of war arrive in the city, invites the audience to imagine a brave new world where children rule, using the best procedures of a democratic society. It is up, then, to the viewer to ask, Were if this just, well-ruled communal society could in fact exist?

The themes of rebirth, redemption and new beginnings are strong in this film, and Mão de Ferro's trajectory as an orphan illustrates all of them. We meet Mão de Ferro very early on and come to understand the type of character he is. The film opens with the sounds of gunshots and children screaming, as they run out of what seems to be a classroom. As chaos ensues and people are killed by the soldiers, we get to see a close up of Mão de Ferro for the first time. He pulls out a ring, brushes the dust off of it, and puts it on a necklace for himself. As one of the soldiers calls out to him, he steps out of a house. He has a diagonal scar across his face and a gun in his hands. It is clear that he is a child-soldier, as he is not much older than the children running from the classroom. The music playing when he steps out of the house is quite menacing, signaling that Mão de Ferro means trouble (his name translates as "Iron Fist"). After a minute of walking with the captured group, he scorns one of the girls for feeding her child. "Next time I'll blow your foot off!" he tells her as he takes the food away from her. Right after this interaction, he goes off in a manic state and starts shooting everywhere around him, blowing up the mines near him and killing several members of the group. He then has a vision of a dog, but it seems to be some sort of mirage. He shoots at the dog, but doesn't seem to hit it at all. In his recklessness, he kills the baby the girl was trying to feed. This occurs within the first few minutes of the film, and is a clear warning to the viewer of the kind of character Mão de Ferro is: he is a product of war; he craves war and violence.

Not long after this first sequence of events, a voice-over informs the audience that only five children survived the war. The following sequence of scenes focuses on those five children who, like ghosts, flee from a devastated rural area and end up arriving in a city run by children who have lost the ability to grow but are learning how to collectively and effectively run their city. As the five orphans travel, the youngest (and thus more innocent and naive) of them sees the children's republic on the horizon and points it out to his fellow companions, but the others do not seem to see it yet. They finally are able to see it and enter, and are welcomed by the young citizens. But the two eldest orphans cannot let go of their hatred for each other, nor their hatred of themselves, as they have been hurt far too much by the civil war. The eldest girl has her baby die right in front of her at the hands of Mão de Ferro, who is hopped up on drugs and a bloodlust that cannot be quenched. Because of their inability to let go of their past and the difficulties of acting as an amicable group, the orphans are nearly banished from the city.

Mão de Ferro cannot seem to snap out of his soldier-like state of mind and he clearly shows signs of post-traumatic stress syndrome. In one scene, when the orphans first enter the city, Mão de Ferro overhears someone say, "Did you see your parents die?" This causes Mão de Ferro to have a flashback to when he was a child. In this flashback, there is blood where his scar now is and a baby cries in the background. He is much younger and looks scared. As he gets up, he is surrounded by dead bodies in a hut and he shakes one of them to see if the person is still alive. The audience then sees the ring that Mão de Ferro took out at the beginning of the film. He takes it off of the hand of a body which can be assumed to be that of his dead mother. A soldier then comes into the hut, grabs Mão de Ferro, and takes him away from the hut. In this flashback scene, the audience finds out about the horrors that Mão de Ferro had to face as a child. Just like Ndala, he witnesses the murder of his family and is taken away from his home. Unlike Ndala, who is taken away by the nuns for reasons of safety, Mão de Ferro is taken away to be trained as a soldier. One can say that, regarding the representation of war and violence, Gomes' film is much more brutal and rawer than *A Cidade Vazia*.

Gomes's use of orphanhood in *Republica di Mininus* speaks to the traumatic experience of the war and the guilt of participating in it, but, above all, to the hope of rebuilding societies so that they will be oriented by collective values rather than individual interests (which was an overarching idea that motivated twentieth century utopias). One can say that the orphans who collaborate in the creation of this new *Republica* embody the African continent in search of new forms of political parenthood, while avoiding the mistakes of the past and reinventing cultural traditions. The audience can thus interpret the long Carnival[13] sequence as a mockery not only of the colonial past but also the international and national political ideologies and practices that have led to the country's mismanagement, and at the same time as a celebration of new forms of governance, in which the younger generations have the lead role: "youth, childhood and fantasy" are central elements in Gomes' filmography, since "the

---

[13] The symbolic meaning of this scene has been flagged up by Ute Fendler: "The children, who organize a parade, present national and international politics with laughter, as a comedy of rogues. At the same time, the utopian setting of the children's republic seems realistic, beside the spectacle of international politics. The film therefore approaches Mikhail Bakhtin's concept of the carnivalesque, which essentially means abolishing the social hierarchy in order to allow an open and constructive criticism of power and the proposing of alternatives." (2019, p. 45).

future belongs to the younger generations, with the ability to reinvent problematic, weighty legacies in a more positive terms" (Passos 2019, 123).

Gomes' film depicts a scenario in which faith and hope inspire the younger generations to abandon old practices of government and to build a new political and organizational reality. While maintaining an agenda focused on furthering a national identity, Gomes offers a transnational vision of the country, as if saying that Guinea-Bissau's political instability is not an isolated case in Africa.[14] The anonymity of the location (the film was actually shot in Mozambique) and the use of English in this film contribute to Gomes' transnational and humanistic approach. [15] Moreover, inspired by the revolutionary figure of Amílcar Cabral, Gomes insists in his films on the compatibility of African traditions and new tools and ideas offered by the contemporary world.[16] The glasses found by Nunta – the young doctor of the city respected by all of the children and mentored by the only adult present there – in the basement of the presidential palace, during the bombardment of the city, symbolically lead back to the figure of Cabral. As an embodiment of Cabral's sociopolitical values, Nunta's mentor, played by American actor Danny Glover, is the only adult involved in the construction of this republic and not by chance his name – Dubem – refers to a person who is good, a person of good values and intentions (*"uma pessoa do bem"*).

In a comparative analysis, Mão de Ferro does not lose his innocence, as Ndala does. He has already lost it when the audience meets him. Having killed and seen killings, he is completely damaged by the war, but he is granted an opportunity to liberate himself – the sequence of scenes in which he is invited

---

[14] This dual dimension has been well explored by Akin Adesokan in his article "Flora Gomes: Filmmaker in Search of a Nation" (2011).
[15] For the purpose of this essay, I will not focus on the debate around the definitions of national and transnational cinema, specially so because both films analyzed here, while dealing with local problems, invite us to openly reflect on a reality that goes beyond a national dimension. My use of "transnational" is informed by Paulo de Medeiros' proposal: "Lusophone cinemas should be understood as a transnational cinemas, on the basis of their funding, the choice of actors, the profile of the film makers who themselves are often transnational, and further, in the way they criticize and problematize their respective societies and dialogue with other films and literary works." (2019, p. 23).
[16] It is interesting to notice that the same reconciliation can be found in literary works. For instance, referring to the short stories complied on A Escola by Domingas Samy, Martin Neumann observes that "os textos literários da Guiné-Bissau (…) visam uma espécie de reconciliação entre as tradições (como elementos da identidade Africana) em mudança e as exigências do mundo moderno" ("the literary texts of Guinea-Bissau (…) aim at a kind of reconciliation between the changing traditions (as elements of African identity) and the demands of the modern world" 2017, p. 134, my translation)

to play soccer for the first time illustrates the beginning of his rebirth as a child. The second moment of redemption happens when Dubem guides Mão de Ferro and the rest of the group to the path of forgiveness and rehabilitation through a ritual reminiscent of baptism. Mão de Ferro emerges from this ceremony with the scar that we see on his face throughout the film completely gone, which suggests that his scarred past has been absolved and that he no longer sees himself as the deformed monster the scar made him out to be. Unlike the bad role model Joka represents in *A Cidade Vazia*, and the group of adults running the country at the beginning of *Republica di Mininus* who focus on nothing but money, power, and violence, Dubem gives the children a foundation of good traits and skills that they can build on.

Slowly corrupted by Luanda, which is itself corrupted by the ongoing violence of the civil war, Ndala loses his innocence and dies at the hands of the man he is robbing on behalf of Joka. Ndala loses his innocence by dying. The children of the republic – and more specifically the protagonist – have already lost theirs, having witnessed bloodshed and suffered the deaths of loved ones. But while Ndala is unable to see the danger posed by Joka, the children that make up the new republic are able to protect themselves and use their skills to benefit one another, inspired by Dubem's words: "the future changes every second, it is the present that matters."

Both *A Cidade Vazia* and *Republica di Mininus* contain stories that revolve around the effects of war on children, showcasing opposite outcomes for orphaned characters. Ndala and Mão de Ferro have both seen the horrors of war. In *A Cidade Vazia*, Ndala is taken from his homeland of Bié by missionaries, after having witnessed the murder of his family. Ndala is lucky to get out alive, but he does not really seem to fully grasp the gravity of the situation. His innocence makes him take literally what the nuns have said about his parents now belonging to the sky, and leads him reject the possibility of finding a permanent place to live. For instance, when Zé tells Ndala that he can be safe in Luanda instead of going back to where there is a war, he reiterates his desire to find his way home. The children in the new republic, from the beginning, offer the new group food, water, shelter, and even a permanent place to stay if they can show they fit in with the community. Mão de Ferro knows this, and yet, he still causes trouble, which discourages the young citizens from continuing to welcome him. In both films, the two orphan characters reject the idea of a new family. Ndala seems to be naive about the good and bad influences around him, while Mão de Ferro purposely rejects positive influences, while embracing recklessness. However, Mão de Ferro's fate is the complete opposite of Ndala's, as he is ultimately made aware of the advantages of playfulness and friendship by people around him. The scene where he passes out after seeing the menacing dog for the last time is a turning point in his path of redemption, and this moment acquires symbolic meaning in the rebirth ritual. Following Dubem's guidance, the five members of the group are invited to throw stones – that they have previously gathered while thinking about their bad misdeeds, sorrows, and griefs – into the ocean. The ritual seems to be effective for Mão de Ferro. As he throws the stones into the water, he says to himself, "Free me of this weight." He later takes off his soldier's uniform and runs into the ocean. The children come to grab the uniform and they bury it in the sand. As Mão de Ferro enters the water, he disappears. He reappears as he runs back onto the land, free of his scar forever. This sequence can, thus, be interpreted as the performance of a religious ceremony where pardon comes after confession, and rebirth comes after a ritual of purification.

There is another relevant point to be made. Mão de Ferro's rebirth and, consequently, the creation of his new family doesn't happen as the five children's journey begins. As the children wander in search of a place to live, the camera travels with them, showing them together but not as a cohesive group yet. The camera shows them from the front, back, and side; and it shows individual close-ups and long sequences of the children walking creating the impression of time passing and portraying the devastation of the territory. Even after their arrival in the city, the children are not presented as a cohesive group; rather, what all the shots and framing emphasize is the lack of union and interpersonal connection between them. It is only in one of the last scenes, which precedes the final panoramic view of the water and the trees, confirming the rebirth ritual, that the audience sees the children posing as a family group. Deeply traumatized by the death of his family and the spiral of violence he sees himself involved in, and addicted to drugs to ease his pain, Mão de Ferro only finds peace after letting go of his past and his losses, finally embracing his new reality among the other many orphans.

Mão de Ferro's emergence from the sea symbolizes his regeneration. He enters the city a war-torn child who knows nothing but violence. He comes out of the ocean a new child, one ready to move forward and embrace the love and friendship bestowed on him by others. His transformation journey from the beginning of the film to the end is almost the complete opposite of Ndala's. Ndala is innocent about the war and violence and about the dangers of Luanda, when he decides to run away from the nuns and his peers. He finds love and friendship through a false idol in Joka. Because of this and his naive nature, but mostly because of a lack of guidance, he is unable to embrace a true path towards good. Mão de Ferro, on the other hand, at first rejects the love and guidance he is offered. Once he comes to terms with his self-hatred and realizes the travesty of violence, he is able to be guided towards a bright future. Ganga's pessimistic view of Luanda's urban space, derived from the emptiness of societal values and the lack of positive and transformative role models in the aftermath of a destructive civil war, contrasts radically with Gomes's optimistic reinvention of the social and political space.

Final Remarks

The devastation and emptiness portrayed in *Republica de Mininus* are seen as essential to a much-desired rebirth of postcolonial African societies. Contrary to Ganga, who envisions orphanhood as a fatal state of being, Gomes projects a hopeful and transformative, perhaps even utopian, view of orphanhood. Unlike the dystopian view of Ganga regarding Angola's future, which is deeply marked by the aftermath of the fratricidal war, Gomes uses the trope of the orphan as a key element for re-imagining the political world and re-acquiring a political voice in the African postcolonial context, particularly in Guinea-Bissau. The condition of orphanhood depicted by Gomes is far from naive, if one believes that only a state of orphanhood would truly allow the postcolonial subject to cut ties with the violent past, the social and political vicious dynamics as well as the strong ethnic and social divisions that have been harming Guinea-Bissau's political stability and social peace. In *Republica de Mininus*, the orphan is instrumental in advertising and investigating alternative social bonds that can posit an effective democratic society. These bonds that go beyond the neocolonial institutions are, thus, powerful tools with which to approach trauma and loss. In this sense, the successful transformation of the orphan suggests the possibility of recreating the devastated country, and shows a way forward.

In both films, the viewer is offered an open criticism of the political elites that ignore and/or do not address the suffering of the impoverished population. In Ganga's film this criticism is taken to the extreme with the portrait of Luanda's street violence and the complete abandonment of the war orphans whose last resource is surviving through crime. Produced during the civil conflict, Ganga cannot imagine a way out for the Angolan society. Filmed almost a decade after, the criticism of the political elite in the *Republica di Mininus* is done through an allegory. The "were if" created by Gomes invites a reflection about a sense of mission and ethical responsibility among all the citizens. Everyone is invited to look after one another and to make each other accountable. The reception of the five war orphans in this unique republic is indicative of an empathetic decision of taking care of the impoverished subjects with the ultimate goal of rescuing and liberating them from the cycle of violence. The adults who interact with Ndala in Luanda are trapped in their own selfishness and therefore are unable to care for others. To the disillusioned vision of the future presented by Maria João Ganga, Flora Gomes depicts the failure of the State in favor of the power of agency of the young generation and, by doing that, he creates the ultimate sense of hope, even if through a utopian lens. The orphaned children become, in Gomes's *Republica*, the bearers of the future.

Works Cited

Arenas, Fernando. *Lusophone Africa. Beyond Independence*. Minneapolis: University of Minnesota Press, 2011.

Fendler, Ute. "African Cinema: A Transnational Cinema? The Decolonial Cinema of Flora Gomes." *Postcolonial Nation and Narrative III: Literature & Cinema*. Eds. Ana M. Leite, Hilary Owen, Ellen W. Sapega and Carmen Tindó Secco. Oxford: Peter Lang, 2019, 35-50.

Ferreira, Carolin Overhoff. *Identity and Difference. Postcoloniality and Transnationality in Lusophone Films*. LIT Verlag, 2012.

Floyd, William David. *Orphans of British fiction, 1880-1911*. Diss. University of Stirling, 2011.

Kimball, Melanie. "From Folktales to Fiction: Orphan Characters in Children's Literature." *Librarytrends*. Vol. 47, n. 3, Winter 1999, 558-578.

König, Eva. *Orphan in Eighteenth-Century Fiction: The Vicissitudes of the Eighteenth- Century*. Palgrave Macmillan, 2014.

Leite, Ana Mafalda. "Introduction." *Postcolonial Nation and Narrative III: Literature & Cinema*. Eds. Ana M. Leite, Hilary Owen, Ellen W. Sapega and Carmen Tindó Secco. Oxford: Peter Lang, 2019, 1-17.

Lopes, António Soares. "Guiné-Bissau – Os Caminhos da Liberdade e da Democracia. Do êxito retumbante ao fracasso. *Rethinking Postcolonialism – Rutura, Transgressão e Transformação nas Literaturas Lusófonas de África*. Eds. Martin Neumann; Marita Rainsborough, Edições Colibri, 2015, 87-98.

Medeiros, Paulo de. "Lusophone Cinemas in Transnational Perspective." *Postcolonial Nation and Narrative III: Literature & Cinema*. Eds. Ana M. Leite, Hilary Owen, Ellen W. Sapega and Carmen Tindó Secco. Oxford: Peter Lang, 2019, 21-33.

Neumann, Martin. "Nas margens da periferia? O conto guineense." *Forma Breve*, "O conto: o cânone e as margens," n.º 14, 2017, 339-357.

Oliviera, Jusciele. "'I make films to be seen': the narrative issue of Flora Gomes." *Journal of Science and Technology of the Arts*. Vol 11, n.1, 2019, 1-10.

___. O filme será um element original da arte negra? Sobre os finais metafórios dos films africanus de Flora Gomes. *Revista da ABPN*. Vol. 11, n. 27, 2018-2019, 11-37.

Passos, Joana. "Flora Gomes: Resilient Hope on Scant Chances." *Postcolonial Nation and Narrative III: Literature & Cinema*. Eds. Ana M. Leite, Hilary Owen, Ellen W. Sapega and Carmen Tindó Secco. Oxford: Peter Lang, 2019, 123-143.

Parvulescu, Constantin. *Orphans of the East: postwar Eastern European cinema and the revolutionary subject*. Indianapolis Indiana University Press, 2015.

Punnett, Audrey. *The Orphan: A Journey to Wholeness*. Fisher King Press, 2014.

Tavares, Ana Paula. *O Lago da Lua*. Lisbon: Caminho, 1999.

Troy, Maria Holmgren, KELLA, Elizabeth, and WAHLSTRÖM, Helena. *Making home: Orphanhood, Kinship, and Cultural Memory in Contemporary American Novels*. Manchester University Press, 2014.

UKADIKE, N. Frank. "In Guinea-Bissau, cinema trickles down: an interview with Flora Gomes." *Research in African Literatures.* Vol. 26, n. 3, 1995, 179-185.

Filmography

A Cidade Vazia. Dir. Maria João Ganga. Prod. Integrada Produções, François Gonot, Animatografo 2. Script: Maria João Ganga. Angola and Portugal, 2004. DVD.

Republica di Mininus. Dir. Flora Gomes. Prod. François Artemare, Maria João Mayer. Script: Flora Gomes, Frank Moisnard. Les films de l'Après-Midi; Filmes do Tejo. Guinea-Bissau, France and Portugal, 2012. DVD.

Chapter 7

Cabo Verde from Text to Silver Screen: Germano Almeida's *The Last Will and Testament of Senhor da Silva Araújo*

David Mongor-Lizarrabengoa

Wor-Wic Community College in Salisbury, Maryland

Abstract

In this chapter, I examine the 1989 Cabo Verdean novel *O Testamento do Sr. Napumoceno da Silva Araújo* (The Last Will and Testament of Senhor da Silva Araújo) written by Germano Almeida and the 1997 film adaptation directed by Francisco Manso, which was a co-production between Cabo Verde, Brazil , and Portugal. Using intertextuality and other theories in the field of adaptation studies, I examine how this seemingly uncinematic novel was made into a feature film that highlights the culture of Cabo Verde. I also analyze its status as a co-production; in doing so, I argue many aspects of the novel were modified to fit the best interests of the co-producing countries. These changes include the use of actors from Brazil (instead of Cabo Verdean ones), the exploration of race (which is absent in the novel), and the roles of women. As a result, the film has a broader appeal to the Lusophone world as a whole instead of being a film geared towards a Cabo Verdean audience. This system is not unique to Cabo Verde; it is relevant to other third world nations with small film industries that attempt to adapt literary texts.

Keywords: Cabo Verde, Germano Almeida, Francisco Manso, adaptation studies

* * *

Much like the other nations represented in this volume, Cabo Verdean [1]literary texts and cinema have not received as much critical attention from scholars compared to other Lusophone nations. Unlike Portugal and Brazil, both of which have had extensive literary production for hundreds of years, the same cannot be said for Cabo Verde. As David Brookshaw explains, "Cape Verdean literature…was born in the twentieth century, and for some time, could be considered to have been the vanguard of the emerging African literatures in Portuguese" (Brookshaw 1996, 179). Obviously, many factors have shaped the literary scene on the islands in the second half of the twentieth century, most notably the 1974 coup in Portugal which, in part, led to Cabo Verde's fight for independence and literary magazines such as *Claridade*[2], *Raízes*[3], and *Ponto & Vírgula*.

The focus of this chapter will be on Germano Almeida's 1989 novel *O Testamento do Sr. Napumoceno Silva de Araújo* and the 1997 film adaptation *O Testamento do Senhor Napumoceno* directed by Francisco Manso. Without a doubt, literary texts have served as major sources of inspiration for directors and filmmakers since the birth of cinema. Clearly, some novels and stories are well-suited for the silver screen as the source texts are highly cinematographic. For example, Gabriel García Márquez's novella, *The Incredible and Sad Tale of Innocent Eréndira and Her Heartless Grandmother* was easily adapted into a 1983 film titled *Eréndira* by Mozambican-born director Ruy Guerra. According to Bell-Villada, the "story in fact was first drafted in 1968 as a film script" (Bell-Villada 2010, 198); the original script was lost, and it is believed García Márquez recalled it from memory. In addition, García Márquez, who had studied cinematography in Italy, co-wrote the screenplay of *Eréndira* which likely made the transition to screen easier. On the other hand, there are plenty of texts that are very uncinematic which will pose a challenge for a director seeking to adapt them for moviegoers. García Márquez's masterpiece, *One Hundred Years of Solitude*, would fall into this second category as filming the novel would be extremely difficult. In an interview titled "Tales Beyond Solitude", García Márquez stated that he wrote *One Hundred Years of Solitude* "against the cinema."

---

[1] On October 25th, 2013, Cabo Verde changed its official English name at the United Nations from Cape Verde. Throughout this chapter I will use the name Cabo Verde, but will use Cape Verde when citing sources that predate the island nation's name change.

[2] For more information on *Claridade*, see Norman Araujo's chapter titled "The Review Entitled *Claridade*" in <u>Critical Perspectives on Lusophone African Literature</u>.

[3] For more information on *Raízes*, see Norman Araujo's chapter titled "New Directions in Cape Verdean Literature? The First Numbers of Raízes" in <u>Critical Perspectives on Lusophone African Literature</u>.

While very different from García Márquez's novel, *O Testamento do Sr. Napumoceno Silva de Araújo* would also qualify as a very uncinematic text. The story focuses on the reading of da Silva Araújo's three hundred- and eighty-seven-page last will and testament. The notary tasked with reading the will even jokes, "he complained that the deceased, thinking he was drafting his will, had instead written his memoirs" (Almeida 2004, 1). While reading the will, the stories that da Silva Araújo includes were often exaggerated to boast his own character and accomplishments, or written in his later years when his mind had deteriorated to the point that he was likely writing pure fiction or simply writing down events he imagined in delirium. The remaining part of the novel focuses on the distribution of the late man's property, specifically his daughter trying to locate his long-lost lover (who may not have existed) to give her a book. The nonlinear flow of the novel as well as the events of the plot that may seem mundane to some undoubtedly pose a challenge for a director hoping to adapt a novel written by one of Cabo Verde's most prominent contemporary writers that viewers will find engaging and want to watch that also captures some of the essences of the source text. The focus of this chapter will analyze how Manso creates an engaging film based on an uncinematic text with specific attention to the female protagonists that play major roles in da Silva Araújo's life. The novel, indisputably, leaves many questions and gaps about Napumoceno and Cabo Verde as a whole. Can Manso's adaptation provide us with any answers? Can it help readers better understand Almeida's novel? What can studying adaptations tell us about film production?

Adaptation Theory

Before diving into Almeida's novel and Manso's film, it is pertinent to discuss the methodology used here in analyzing film adaptations as there have been many different approaches presented since George Bluestone's book *Novels into Film*, the first major publication to address the issue, was released in 1957. The intention here is not to propose a new theory on how to critically examine the relationship between a source text and its adaptation; rather, the goal is to use different ideas and theories proposed by various scholars to dissect the complex relationship between the two works. One important factor to keep in mind is that the novel and cinema use completely different semiotic systems, the written word and visual image respectively. Robert Stam, in his essay "Beyond Fidelity: The Dialogics of Adaptation", explains, "Each medium has its own specificity deriving from its respective materials of expression. The novel has a single medium of expression, the written word, whereas the film has at least five tracks: moving photographic image, phonetic sound, music, noises, and written materials" (Stam 2000, 59). As such, it is erroneous when anybody attempts to make a hierarchal comparison of the two. When any director and screenwriter decide to attempt to adapt a piece of fiction into a film, they must realize that it is not possible to be completely faithful to the source text. Viewers of the movie should also not expect strict fidelity either as the book and film are in different mediums. "No matter how concrete and specific an author's diction, his or her verbal language is ultimately unfixed and unspecified" (Desmond & Hawkes 2017, 35). The images on screen are fixed and specific as a director and his/her crew have to make creative decisions on how to present the source material. These choices will likely be different from the mental images a reader comes up with upon reading that particular section.

Way too often, the issue of fidelity comes up when film adaptations are examined by the academic community and casual viewing public. Brian McFarlane asserts, "Discussion of adaptation has been bedeviled by the fidelity issue" (McFarlane 2004, 8). In "Adaptation, or the Cinema as Digest", Bazin explains that film adaptations should focus more on "the *equivalence in meaning of the forms*" (Bazin 2000, 20) instead of how faithful the movie is to the book in terms of the plot. Simply pointing out the similarities and differences between the two is uninteresting and offers little in terms of critical analysis. Instead, there is promise in Julia Kristeva's concept of intertextuality. Intertextuality is "the transposition of one or more systems of signs into another, accompanied by a new articulation of the enunciative and denotative position" (Roudiez 1980, 15). Kristeva explains that "authors do not create their texts from their own original minds, but rather compile them from pre-existent texts, so that... a text is 'a permutation of texts, an intertextuality in the space of a given text', in which 'several utterances, taken from other texts, intersect and neutralize on another'" (Allen 2011, 35). Robert Stam sees intertextuality as a useful approach to analyzing literary texts and film adaptations. According to Stam:

> In the broadest sense, intertextual dialogism refers to the infinite and open-ended possibilities generated by all the discursive practices of a culture, the entire matrix of communicative utterances within which the artistic text is situated, which read not only through recognizable influences, but also through a subtle process of dissemination. (Stam 2000, 64)

As suggested by Stam and other critics, intertextuality is a useful approach when examining any aspects of film adaptations as it, for starters, offers a much more informative and analytical approach compared to examining the issue of fidelity. As an art form, films borrow heavily from literary texts, television shows, plays, other films, and all sorts of visual arts; therefore, intertextuality becomes a logical lens in which one can analyze a film.

Germano Almeida & Cabo Verdean Literature

Almeida, without a doubt, emerged in the late 1980s with the publication of *O Testamento do Sr. Napumoceno Silva de Araújo* and his third[4] novel, *O meu Poeta* (1991) as Cabo Verde's most prolific modern author. To date, he has published sixteen books, nine of which are novels. Scholars of Luso-African literature often consider him to Cabo Verde what Mia Couto is for Mozambique and Pepetela is to Angola. His works have achieved great success in Cabo Verde, other Lusophone nations, and even the United States. Russell Hamilton argues that Almeida's international recognition is due, in part, to his presentation of Cabo Verdean, Creole, and African culture. In his words:

> Almeida has made clever use of the...chronicle, which in Portuguese-speaking world has become a unique genre with elements of quotidian history as well as op-ed provocation... [He] historicizes and sensationalizes the uniqueness of Cape Verdean identity and the archipelago's paradoxically central and peripheral location. (Hamilton 2010, 33)

In many cases, after a nation gains independence from its colonizers, artists of different mediums tend to reject previous movements and models. Often, this is done in an effort to establish a unique identity instead of simply copying or imitating what has been previously produced or is being written elsewhere. This is definitely the case with Cabo Verde in the 1990s, "Cape Verdean...prose fiction also ventured forth into satire and parody, a factor possibly explained by the political opening which occurred around 1990" (Brookshaw 1996, 188).

Up until the late twentieth century, there were a few main themes that dominated Cabo Verde's literary production, which mostly involved its geography. The islands that comprise Cabo Verde are situated between 320 and 460 nautical miles west of Senegal's Cap-Vert Peninsula. This position made them an ideal location/stopover for shipping routes, but the 1,577 square miles of land lack natural resources. The nonexistence of natural resources, undoubtedly, caused a shortage of lucrative jobs on the islands in the twentieth century so emigrating to Portugal, the United States, other parts of West Africa, and some Western European nations. On top of this, extreme weather conditions, most notably drought, also affected the desire for Cabo Verdeans to seek opportunities abroad. "Statistical analyses demonstrate that being unemployed, having relatives abroad, and receiving remittances are factors

---

[4] Almeida's first novel, *O dia das calças roladas*, was published in 1982, but it has not had the same critical success as *O Testamento do Sr. Napumoceno Silva de Araújo* or *O meu Poeta.*

that contribute to the wish to emigrate…The widespread desire to emigrate cannot be explained exclusively by economic or demographic factors. The idea of emigration and return as a path to prosperity is a deeply rooted aspect of Cape Verdean society" (Carling 2017). In addition, Rothwell and Martinho explain, "Cabo Verde…has often seen its island status as a source of isolation and difference, as well as creating a nexus linking it to a diaspora around the globe" (Rothwell and Martinho 2016, 2). Regardless of the causes and reasons for emigration, it, along with geographical factors like droughts, were prominent themes in Cabo Verdean literature until the late twentieth century.

Upon gaining independence from Portugal, Cabo Verde's government sought to expand cultural production in the nation; however, there were many other challenges that the new country faced. Passos explains the first republic government:

> tried to promote literary creation by organising contests and awards. However, most postcolonial literary production has been published in local newspapers and magazines… Committed writers keep underlining the necessity of a more systematic investment in publishing and culture (Passos 2003, 158)

Things, however, started to change with Almeida and his contemporaries as there was a shift to sort of re-invent / re-present the image of Cabo Verde's depiction in literary texts. From their perspectives, the nation is much more than a group of islands plagued by drought and where there is a strong culture of finding prosperity abroad. With specific regard to *O Testamento do Sr. Napumoceno Silva de Araújo* and *O meu Poeta*, Brookshaw states:

> Both of these works have propelled Cape Verdean fiction into the forefront of literary post-modernism. They reflect a reaction against the oppression of one monolithic truth, a desire to interpret rather than merely describe island reality, and above all to analyse the new society which has emerged since 1975. (Brookshaw 1996, 188)

As Brookshaw suggests, Almeida seeks to uncover the roots and find the true essence of Cabo Verdean society as opposed to a surface-level depiction of how life has evolved on the islands in the decades following the nation's independence from Portugal and to universalize what it is like to be a Cabo Verdean.

Adapting the Novel: The Written Word

In the case of *O Testamento do Sr. Napumoceno Silva de Araújo*, the written word, in various forms, is central to the story. As stated previously, the written word is the primary way a printed text conveys its messages; films are multitracked and use much more than written words to communicate points to viewers. One of the reasons why one could consider Almeida's novel to be uncinematic is due to the importance of the two texts that inform readers about da Silva Araújo's life: his 387-page will and the school notebooks he specifically left to his daughter Graça which reveal details of his life that were not discussed in the will. While these two texts are central to the novel, the act of writing itself has a much deeper role. As Rothwell explains:

> Writing exerts a primacy throughout the discoveries made by Graça...in regard to her father. From the will itself, to her father's notebooks, to the piece of paper discovered by...Dona Eduarda with the name Adélia written and then punctured as if in a desperate act of scriptural expiation, the written word is allied with the creation of this Cape Verdean father's identity. (Rothwell 2007, 97)

Without a doubt, Rothwell is correct in stating the importance of writing to the story as a whole and specifically the relationship between Napumoceno and his daughter. Placing such importance on the written word and various texts would, undoubtedly, be a challenge for a director to recreate on the silver screen but not totally impossible. The piece of paper with Adélia's name could be easily recreated by any director in a single shot. The lengthy will and notebooks are where the challenge arises. In the case of the novel, the reading of the will is described in the first three pages that comprise the first chapter. It is clear that the notary, Carlos, and Sr. Fonesca struggle to get through the formality of reading the will. In Almeida's words, "When he reached the one-hundred-and-fiftieth page, the notary admitted he was already tired and actually broke off to ask that someone bring him a glass of water...he complained that the deceased, think he was drafting his will, had instead written his memoirs" (Almedia 2004, 1). With such a lengthy will, which contains many important pieces of information about Napumoceno's life; it takes the men until 6:30, with minimal interruptions, to finish reading the document. Manso's film does an excellent job at conveying the drawn-out reading of the will. A voiceover begins to tell of some events in Napumoceno's life; there are multiple voices heard including Napumoceno's and that of the mayor of São Nicolau among others. The montage alternates between shots of the clock as time passes with that of the faces of the notary, Fonesca, and Carlos. The close-ups show their reactions of laughter and fatigue to hearing the contents of the will. Chico Díaz, the actor who portrays Carlos, masterfully recreates the reaction written in Almeida's text. Overall, the film does an excellent job recreating the reading of the will/first chapter of the text.

It is important to note, before diving any further into an analysis, that the novel does not contain many excerpts from Napumoceno's will; rather the events that are described in the will are recounted by an omniscient narrator and sometimes by the protagonists themselves. The same is true for the stories described in the notebooks; however, in one of the most notable changes to the source text, the film replaces the notebooks with cassette tapes. When Graça begins to listen to one of the cassette tapes, usually there is a voiceover featuring Napumoceno's voice as he recounts the actions that will be featured in the flashback. Much like the scenes of the reading of the will, these sequences flow well within the context of the overall story and even engage the audience; viewers hear the exact same voice as Graça. This seemingly small modification seems to undermine the importance of the written word in Almeida's novel. "The effect is to reduce the potency of the written" (Rothwell 2007, 96). Obviously, Manso could have made the choice to keep the notebooks and include close-up shots of Napumoceno's words; however, it likely would not have been as effective. The handwritten text would have had to have been large enough so the film viewers would be able to read it, and it would have been necessary for the shot to remain on the screen for several seconds to allow for adequate time to read said text. While this alteration, which may seem minor on the surface, definitely weakens the power and parental connection of the written word as suggested by Rothwell, Manso's change to the audiotapes still manages to convey the same message. Using a voiceover and allowing Graça and the audience to hear Napumoceno's voice was undoubtedly one of the best ways in which Manso could have recreated the notebooks from the novel.

Adapting the Novel: Napumoceno's Women

Without a doubt, the two most important women in Napumoceno's life are Adélia and Graça. One could argue that Chica could be included here as she is, after all, the mother of his daughter. However, given that he tried to pressure her into aborting the baby and then provided her with a pension to ensure she would keep his identity as the father a secret, one could argue that she did not mean a whole lot to him. In addition, Dona Jóia may also carry a special place in Napumoceno's heart as he really enjoyed the time the two spent together, but various distractions prevented their relationship from blossoming into something serious. Beyond these five aforementioned women, Napumoceno encountered other women, primarily in brothels, as he was known to frequent them. On the whole, the novel tends to portray a patriarchal society as women are often seen as mere objects and their voices are silenced.

In the novel, the narrator and Napumoceno serve as the primary voices, and, as such the events of the story are told through their perspective. Carlos and Fonesca occasionally add some details or minor interpretations of events, but their voices never become the dominant ones. When trying to actually unwrap the madness and eccentricities of Napumoceno through these male characters/voices, readers are left with more questions than answers. Yet, if some of the women that played a part in Napumoceno's life had the chance to speak, many unanswered questions could finally be put to bed. For instance, Chica does not say much about Napumoceno to his daughter other than that he is a good man and can be trusted. Given her time working for his company and the arrangements of her pregnancy and pension, she likely could add some more to the portrait we get of Napumoceno. In addition, Dona Eduarda, Napumoceno's maid and housekeeper in his later years, would likely be able to answer some of the questions regarding Napumoceno and Adélia, as she was working and caring for him at the time the two were dating. Eduarda saw first-hand how happy Napumoceno was to be with Adélia and how crushed he was when she left him. Graça questions Eduarda about Adélia, but she says she does not know much, probably because Napumoceno and Adélia spent time together away from his home. It is possible that out of respect for Napumoceno, she does not reveal any information about her former boss's love life, but Eduarda could, undoubtedly, tell Graça about other aspects of Napumoceno's life after he stepped out of the public life. However, as a caretaker, Eduarda would likely be in a lower social class; that, combined with her being a woman would cause her voice to be silenced in a male-dominated, patriarchal society.

Adélia, without a doubt, could also shed light on what Napumoceno is like. Graça is more likely motivated to find Adélia to learn about her father, rather than just to deliver the copy of António Nobre's book of poems titled *Só* (Alone). The contents of Napumoceno's will and the notebooks he left to Graça, for obvious reasons, cannot be taken as the absolute truth, but it is clear that Napumoceno and Adélia spent a lot of time together in his later years. Carlos and Fonesca remember Adélia, but they did not have a very favorable opinion of her like Napumoceno. They, however, did not know her to any great extent. Within the film, Adélia is played by Karla Leal[5], a lighter-skinned woman of color. According to her page on the International Movie Database, she only starred in *Napumoceno's Will* and one other short film in 2005. Again, while sexuality and the female body are often highlighted in modern Brazilian films;

---

[5] In searching the web and other academic sources, little information can be found on Karla Leal. While her background and ethnicity cannot be verified by a reliable source, she is likely Brazilian, like most of the cast, based on how she sounds when speaking Portuguese.

this is not really the case here with Adélia. Given that in the novel, Napumoceno and her have limited sexual engagements, likely due to his inability to satisfy her given his older age, it comes as no surprise that she is not exposed in great detail in Manso's film. What the film seems to lack, when it comes to Adélia and Napumoceno's relationship, is the sequence that Graça finds in one of the notebooks she believes was written at the end of his life due to the penmanship being similar to that of the last portion of the will. While she acknowledges it was most definitely a dream he was writing about as opposed to reality, the events described in chapter six of the novel really highlight the love that Napumoceno had for Adélia. Almeida writes about how Adélia was the main focus of his thoughts for days and her absence was painful to him (Almeida 2004, 99-101). Napumoceno even writes about how Adélia came back to him to be together after she called it quits when her boyfriend returned to the island. While this section of the novel could be hard to recreate for the film, Manso tries to depict Napumoceno's love for Adélia in his final days as he repeatedly calls her name as Dona Eduarda spoon feeds him. Despite the omissions from the text regarding Napumoceno and Adélia's relationship, it should be clear to viewers that he loved her dearly until his passing.

In terms of the visual portrayals of the female protagonists in the film, viewers can see the differences among generations of women. Beginning with Chica, she is shown as a more traditional and conservative woman that would be associated with pre-independence Cabo Verde. Other than the scene in which Napumoceno impregnates her and when she breaks the news of her pregnancy to him, she is always wearing a scarf/bandana. Hair is seen as a symbol of a woman's beauty so covering it prevents her from being seen as a sexual object. However, in the scene from both novel and film when Napumoceno has sex with her, Lopes Gordon argues that he does not even see her as a woman or person at this moment; rather, as that which wears the green skirt, the color associated with his favorite soccer team (Lopes Gordon 2009, 71). As a conservative and more traditional woman with values, for instance, she refuses to abort the child, Manso's visual depiction of her character fits the presentation in Almeida's text.

While Chica's character is not sexualized in the film, this is not the case with other female protagonists. Afro-Brazilian actress, Veluma D'Oba, portrays Chez-Nous in the film, the prostitute and exotic dancer from Dakar, Senegal who gives Napumoceno a sexually transmitted disease after the two sleep together. Nudity is commonplace in many Brazilian films as their society is more accepting of a naked female body compared to certain Western cultures, but there is more at play in the film than just her nudity. In the scene where she makes her first appearance, she performs a dance and song while slowly undressing until being completely topless. The camera alternates between shots of Chez-Nous and the audience reacting to her routine. Napumoceno is among the members of the audience, along with some sailors who are wearing uniforms nearly identical to those worn by members of the United States Navy and other seemingly wealthy members of Cabo Verde's elite. The people in the audience watching Chez-Nous are white. As will be explained in greater detail in the next section, race is not something that Almeida focuses on to any great extent in the novel. Thus, this particular scene of the film appears to suggest that the whites and upper-class in Cabo Verde tend to fetishize African women's bodies. In a subsequent scene, Napumoceno treats Chez-Nous to dinner at what seems to be a high-class restaurant in town. During their meal, the two converse leading to Chez-Nous laughing really loudly much to the distaste of the other restaurant patrons. This scene implies that Chez-Nous is not well-mannered as that sort of conduct is far from befitting in a ritzy establishment. While it is unclear whether or not Manso and his crew wanted to convey any specific message or point through Chez-Nous, her character may seem to be an offensive portrayal of an African woman to some viewers, beyond her simply being a prostitute.

With regard to Dona Jóia, the film expands a bit more on their time together and story than the novel does. While the novel itself has sufficient content for a full-length feature film, Manso chose to add some extra scenes and elements of the story, most likely to better appeal to a Brazilian and wider international audience. Dona Jóia is portrayed by another Brazilian, Elisa Lucinda, who is a light-skinned actress from Cariacica. The movie includes several melodramatic scenes together to illustrate how madly the two fall in love with one another ranging from walks on the beach, to dinner together, and even sex. Towards the end of the film, Graça makes contact with Dona Jóia. Graça learns that Napumoceno had kept writing to Dona Jóia over the years, but he never got any of her responses as Dona Eduarda had intercepted all letters from Dona Jóia; Eduarda thought that Napumoceno would have left Cabo Verde to live in America with Dona Jóia if he knew she still had feelings for him. While it is unclear why Manso added these extra details, it adds a little more melodrama to the film which likely resonated with Brazilian viewers.

Lastly, it is worth discussing Graça's character in the film played by Maria Ceiça. Within the novel, there are a few details about Graça's physical appearance that Manso and his colleagues could have used when choosing actresses to play the part. Almeida writes that Graça had her father's fine black hair, high forehead, and posture. While her mother dresses in more traditional clothing, Graça tends to dress in a much more sophisticated manner, wearing fashionable clothes and pearls (after she inherits her father's estate). Her attire, without a doubt, represents the style of the younger generation of Cabo

Verdeans that grew up when Portugal was losing control of Cabo Verde and when the nation was fully independent.

As already mentioned, the female body can be a major focal point for Brazilian films; thus, it would have been easy for Manso to highlight her sexual features; however, this is not the case. Within the novel, Graça definitely shares her mother's values and respect. Lopes Gordon even argues that she is a "desexualized" character (Lopes Gordon 2009, 74). She possesses her father's physical appearance and business acumen; Graça is determined to continue her father's legacy by keeping the company profitable. Obviously, inheriting such wealth would likely attract some potential suitors, but Almeida does not mention any relationships that Graça had at any point in her life. In a rather odd twist to the plot of the novel, Manso includes a subplot in the film in which Carlos tries to win over Graça romantically despite the pair being related. He attempts to win her over by being very helpful when she has questions and sends her flowers. Whenever she mentions him to other characters in the film, they warn her to be careful and have looks of disgust on their faces. Carlos is more of a Don Juan in the film as he has dates arranged with various women and even tries to pick one up at his uncle's funeral. His pursuit of Graça culminates when he asks her for a kiss in the car while giving her a driving lesson. She agrees to do so only if he tells her why Napumoceno disinherited him. Graça is all about business so she rejects his attempt at affection instead of using the opportunity to try to uncover something Carlos may be hiding. While the inclusion of Carlos's efforts to seduce Graça is odd, it does not distract from the fact she is not sexualized to any extent in the film and maintains the values instilled by her mother and remains the desexualized character that Lopes Gordon observes.

Adapting the Novel: Race and Cabo Verdean Society

Within the novel itself, race is rarely mentioned; the focus is more on gender as the various women that enter Napumoceno's life often play important roles in the narrative. Given that a director needs to pick actors for the main cast and background extras, it is impossible to avoid depicting one race or many. Before discussing the specific actors that Manso and his team chose for the roles, it is worth briefly discussing the racial demographics of Cabo Verde and how its society is portrayed in the novel. As of 2020, the islands have an estimated population of 583,255 with Creole/Mulattos making up the majority of the population at 71%. Africans make up 28%, and Europeans comprise the final 1% of the population (CIA World Factbook). Although these figures represent the current demographic breakdown of Cabo Verde, these percentages have not changed dramatically since Almeida published the novel. Cabo Verdean Creoles/Mulattos came about due to the interracial marriage between the

Africans that were brought to and traveled to the islands and the Portuguese who settled on the islands and eventually established a colony there. As a result, it is not uncommon to see Cape Verdean Creoles with features from both ancestries. In an article published in *Público*, Joana Gorjão Henriques notes, "Cape Verde is not Africa, Cape Verdeans are 'special blacks' and the closest to Portugal. Cape Verde is the country of miscegenation, the 'proof" of 'racial harmony' of Luso-Tropicalism" (Gorjão Henriques 2016). In addition to racial demographics, it is worth noting the poverty rates as well as income-level can have a major impact on how a society functions and often is tied to one's race. According to João Monteiro, in his article, "Human Development, Economic Policy and Income Inequality in Cabo Verde," the country is among the "top development and democratic performers in Africa" (Monteiro 2018, 4). This, however, was not always the case. He notes that in 1988, one year prior to the publication of Almeida's novel, the poverty rate in Cabo Verde was roughly forty-nine percent (Monteiro 2018, 4). Information on the poverty rate and racial makeup of the country is important as Almeida's novel attempts to offer a realistic depiction of Cabo Verde before, during, and in the decade following independence. As such, one would expect to see such diversity in the film adaptation.

Napumoceno's Will was co-produced by Cabo Verde, Brazil, and Portugal. The director, Francisco Manso, is from Portugal. Despite the film being an adaptation of a Cabo Verdean novel, all of the main cast is portrayed by Brazilian actors. As stated at the beginning of this section, Almeida does place any major focus on race; but this is not the case in the film. Napumoceno is played by São Paulo-born actor Nelson Xavier, a white Brazilian. Graça, on the other hand, is portrayed by Maria Ceiça, an Afro-Brazilian actress from Rio de Janeiro. There appears to be no apparent reason for the racial codification of their relationship. No comments from Manso and his casting crew regarding this decision could be found; however, one may speculate that the choice was intentional. In her book, *A primeira elite colonial atlântica: dos "homens honrados brancos" de Santiago à "nobreza da terra": finais do séc. XV - início do séc. XVII*, Iva María Cabral, states," "the Cape Verdean elite thought that they were white" and "superior to the rest of the population" (cited in Gorjão Hernriques 2016). Cabral's comments, combined with the fact that Napumoceno and many of the people of São Vicente in the novel viewed him as one of the most prominent and influential members of the city, an actor who looks white would seem to be the best fit for the role. Additionally, much like his uncle, Carlos also considers himself among the elite of the island. Chico Díaz, a Mexican-born Brazilian actor, plays Carlos in the film; he is also very light-skinned. Obviously, not all members of the Cabo Verdean elite are portrayed by white actors in Manso's movie; rather, his choice of actors is very interesting due to the racial codification as the novel does not specify the ethnic background or skin color of its characters.

With regard to other members of the film's cast, there is a lot of diversity. Vya Negromonte, the actress who portrays María Chica and was the real-life husband of Nelson Xavier, appears as a lighter-skinned African woman in the film. Napumoceno's final servant, Dona Eduarda, is played by Zezé Motta, one of Brazil's most famous black actresses. Another famous black Brazilian actor is in Manso's film; Milton Gonçalves portrays the mayor of São Vicente. The inclusion of Xavier, Motta, and Gonçalves in the movie was likely to broaden the appeal to Brazilian audiences as all three were notable actors in the country. The appearance in the film combined with the various other minor characters of various races and wealth highlight the presence of multiple cultures in Cabo Verde in the 1990s. Within the novel, Napumoceno describes the diverse makeup of São Vicente in a thesis stating the island is made up of natives from some of the other islands who were forced to relocate for various reasons, people influenced by American culture, and people from other regions of the world; this mixing, according to Napumoceno has caused the population of São Vicente to become the most inauthentic of Cape Verdeans (128). While it may pose a challenge for readers to envision the diversity of São Vicente and numerous cultural influences from reading the novel, film viewers have no such issue due to the film being shot on the island and the diverse cast.

Conclusion

Undoubtedly, *O Testamento do Sr. Napumoceno Silva de Araújo* is one of the best novels to come out of Cabo Verde since the late 1980s/early 1990s. Almeida manages to highlight many of the issues that arose in the nation following its independence from Portugal. While the novel may seem uncinematic due to its focus on a lengthy will and the search for answers about Napumoceno's life, Manso manages to create an interesting adaptation that may not manage to resolve the mysteries about Napumoceno, but manages to reveal a lot about Almeida's vision of Cabo Verdean society. As I have attempted to highlight in this chapter, the relationship between a novel and its adaptation is a complex one. Readers of the source text will likely watch the movie with certain expectations based on their reading experience. However, a film adaptation can also influence how we interpret the novel on which it is based. In the case of *O Testamento do Sr. Napumoceno Silva de Araújo*, Manso's film succeeds at reworking the written word, which is fundamental to the novel, into powerful visual images that depict the geography, gender roles, and diversity of Cabo Verde. While Almeida is able to avoid discussing the racial backgrounds of his characters, this would be impossible for a director as he/she needs to choose actors and actresses for each role; as such, race, to a degree, becomes a part of an adaptation. In the case here, examining the backgrounds of the cast reveal another issue at play within Lusophone film production, the influence of Portugal and Brazil. In most cases, directors seek to create feature films that will be commercially successful, but sometimes sacrifices need to be made to gain funding for projects. For Manso, the inclusion of actors from Brazil allowed for the film to garner appeal from audiences in other parts of the Lusophone world and financial backing in the form of a co-production. Regardless of the use of a primarily Brazilian cast over a Cabo Verdean one, the movie is still a fine example of Cabo Verde's film production and offers new critical perspectives on Almeida's novel.

Works Cited

Allen, Graham, *Intertextuality*. New York: Routledge, 2011.

Almeida, Germano. *The Last Will and Testament of Senhor Da Silva Araújo*. Translated by Sheila Faria Glaser. New York, NY: New Directions, 2004.

Bazin, André. "Adaptation, or the Cinema of Digest." Essay. In *Film Adaptation*, edited by James Naremore, 19-27. New Brunswick, NJ: Rutgers UP, 2000.

Bell-Villada, Gene H. *García Márquez: The Man and His Work*. Chapel Hill: University of North Carolina Press, 2010.

Brookshaw, David. "Cape Verde." In *The Post Colonial Literature of Lusophone Africa*, edited by Patrick Chabal, 179–233. London: Hurst & Company, 1996.

"Cabo Verde: CIA World Factbook." Central Intelligence Agency. Central Intelligence Agency. Accessed June 14, 2020. https://www.cia.gov/the-world-factbook/countries/cabo-verde/.

Carling, Jørgen. "Cape Verde: Towards the End of Emigration?" migrationpolicy.org, March 2, 2017. https://www.migrationpolicy.org/article/cape-verde-towards-end-emigration.

Desmond, John M., and Peter Hawkes. *Adaptation: Studying Film and Literature*. Boston, MA: McGraw-Hill Education Create, 2017.

Gorjão Henriques, Joana. "To Be African in Cape Verde Is a Taboo." *Público*, January 3, 2016.

Hamilton, Russell. "Contemporary Cape Verdean Literature." *Transition: An International Review*, no. 103 (October 2010): 26–35.

Lopes Gordon, Maria. "The (Un)Holy Trinity: Women's Protagonism in 'O Testamento Do Sr. Napumoceno Da Silva Araújo.'" *Portuguese Studies* 25, no. 1 (2009): 65–79.

McFarlane, Brian. *Novel to Film: An Introduction to the Theory of Adaptation*. Oxford: Clarendon Press, 2004.

Monteiro, João. "Human Development, Economic Policy AndIncome Inequality in Cabo Verde." *Journal of Cabe Verdean Studies* 3, no. 1 (2018): 3–17.

O Testamento Do Senhor Napumoceno. DVD. Cape Verde: SPIA Media Productions, 1997.

Passos, J.F. "Micro-Universes and Situated Critical Theory: Postcolonial and Feminist Dialogues in a Comparative Study of Indo-English and Lusophone Women Writers," 2003.

Roudiez, Leon. "Introduction" In *Desire in Language: A Semiotic Approach to Literature and Art,* edited by Leon Roudiez., 1-22. New York: Columbia UP, 1980.

Rothwell, Phillip. "Inventing a Lusotropical Father, or, the Neurotic Legacy in Germano Almeida's 'O Testamento Do Senhor Napumoceno.'" *Research in African Literatures* 38, no. 1 (2007): 95–105.

Rothwell, Phillip, and Ana Maria Maritnho. "Four Decades of Independence: The Multiple Cultures of Portuguese-Speaking Africa." *Journal of Lusophone Studies* 1, no. 1 (2016): 1–6.

Stam, Robert. "Beyond Fidelity: The Dialogics of Adaptation." Essay. In *Film Adaptation,* edited by James Naremore, 54–76. New Brunswick, NJ: Rutgers UP, 2000.

___. *Subversive Pleasures: Bakhtin, Cultural Criticism, and Film.* Baltimore, MD: Johns Hopkins Univ. Press, 1996.

Tales Beyond Solitude. Faction Media. The South Bank Show, n.d. http://factionmedia.co.uk/films/talesbeyondsolitude.

About the Contributors

Sarita Naa Akuye Addy

Dr. Sarita Naa Akuye Addy holds a doctorate degree in Hispanic Studies from the University of Western Ontario, Canada. Dr. Addy's works to date can be summed as an exercise in highlighting marginalized African voices and experiences in the African diaspora. Her research work at the doctoral level explored the personal colonial and postcolonial histories of Equatorial Guineans through the novels of Guinean authors living in exile to understand the impact of colonialism on African dictatorship regimes, such as that in Equatorial Guinea.

Her future research works will be focusing on the notions of gender and sexuality in the works of Equatorial Guinea's female authors and would like to explore women's perceptions and reactions to Spanish colonialism in Equatorial Guinea. For the time being, she has turned her attention to anti-racism through her work with the Canadian Center for Diversity and Inclusion.

Margret Chipara

Marget Chipara is an instructor of French and Portuguese in the Faculty of Arts and Humanities at the University of Zimbabwe. She holds a BA (Honours) in French and Portuguese and an MPhil in Mozambican Literature from the University of Zimbabwe. Her research interests include comparative literature, onomastics, gender and sociolinguistics, translation, and Portuguese language studies. She has taught courses on Portuguese History, Lusophone Africa, Literary and Non-Literary Translation, and Luso-African Literature.

Joseph Abraham Levi

Dr. Joseph Abraham Levi 雷祖善博士 holds a Ph.D. in Romance Philology/Linguistics (Portuguese, Italian, and Medieval Spanish) from the University of Wisconsin at Madison. His publications, research, and academic interest cover: African, Islamic, Lusophone, and Sephardic studies. He has taught at the University of Wisconsin-Madison, the University of Georgia, the University of Iowa, Rhode Island College, the University of Hong Kong, and the Universidade de São José in Macau. Since fall 2010, he is affiliated with the George Washington University in Washington, D.C.

Patrícia Martinho Ferreira

Patrícia Martinho Ferreira teaches Portuguese language and Lusophone Literatures and Film at University of Massachusetts Amherst. She holds a B.A. in Modern Languages and Literatures (2005) and a M.A. in Theory and Narrative Analysis (2009) from University of Coimbra (Portugal), an M.Ed. in Teaching Portuguese as Foreign and Second Language from University of Porto (Portugal), and a Ph.D. in Portuguese and Brazilian Studies (2018) from Brown University. She is the author of *Orphans of the Empire: Colonial Legacies in Contemporary Portuguese Literature* (Lisbon, ICS, 2021), and several articles published in Hispania, Journal of Lusophone Studies, among other venues.

David Mongor-Lizarrabengoa

Dr. Mongor-Lizarrabengoa is an Assistant Professor of Spanish at Wor-Wic Community College in Salisbury, Maryland. He holds a BA & MA in Spanish from Montclair State University, an MA in English & an MA in film studies from National University, and a PhD in comparative literature from the University of Western Ontario. His research focuses on representations of trauma and torture in modern Latin American & Brazilian film and fiction, literatures of Lusophone Africa, and adaptation studies. He has presented at over 35 conferences across the United States and Canada.

Martha Mzite

Dr. Martha Mzite is an instructor of French and Portuguese at Manicaland State University of Applied Sciences in Zimbabwe. She holds an Honours BA in French and Portuguese from the University of Zimbabwe, an MA in French Studies from the University of Cape Town, and a PhD in French Studies from Rhodes University. Her research interests include Lusophone Literature, Francophone Literature, and didactics and grammar.

Paulo Rodrigues Ferreira

Paulo Rodrigues Ferreira is a Lecturer of Portuguese at the University of North Carolina at Chapel Hill. Before moving to North Carolina, he taught Portuguese at Queens College and Bronx Community College, in New York. In his Ph.D. thesis, titled "Iberismos, Hispanismos e seus Contrários: Portugal e Espanha (1908-1931)," he focused on the intellectual and cultural relations between Portugal and Spain and analyzed the different concepts of Iberianism. His research also concentrates on topics associated with the idea of cultural crisis and with the decline of the Portuguese colonial empire. Paulo is also the author of a novel titled *Uso Errado da Vida* (2019), published in Portugal.

Daniel F. Silva

Daniel F. Silva is Associate Professor of Luso-Hispanic Studies and Director of the Black Studies Program at Middlebury College, where he is also Director of the Twilight Project and a fellow at the Center for the Comparative Study of Race and Ethnicity as well as a contributing member of the International and Global Studies Program. He is the author *of Embodying Modernity: Race, Gender, and Fitness Culture in Brazil* (University of Pittsburgh Press, 2022), *Anti-Empire: Decolonial Interventions in Lusophone Literatures* (Liverpool University Press, 2018), and *Subjectivity and the Reproduction of Imperial Power: Empire's Individuals* (Routledge, 2015). He is also the co-editor of *Decolonial Destinies: The Post-Independence Literatures of Lusophone Africa* (Anthem Press, Forthcoming); *Emerging Dialogues on Machado de Assis* (Palgrave, 2016); and *Lima Barreto: New Critical Perspectives* (Lexington Books, 2013). He is co-editor of the book series, Anthem Studies in *Race, Power, and Society* with Anthem Press; and has published scholarship in *Hispania, Chasqui,* and *Transmodernity* while also contributing to several edited volumes.

Index

www.ingramcontent.com/pod-product-compliance
Lightning Source LLC
Chambersburg PA
CBHW071132280326
41935CB00010B/1190